THE
POWER
OF
RELIGION

THE
POWER
OF
RELIGION

A Comparative Introduction

—ɱ—

Amanda Porterfield

New York   Oxford
OXFORD UNIVERSITY PRESS
1998

Oxford University Press

Oxford New York
Athens Auckland Bangkok Bogota Bombay Buenos Aires
Calcutta Cape Town Dar es Salaam Delhi Florence Hong Kong
Istanbul Karachi Kuala Lumpur Madras Madrid Melbourne
Mexico City Nairobi Paris Singapore Taipei Tokyo Toronto Warsaw

and associated companies in
Berlin Ibadan

Copyright © 1998 by Oxford University Press, Inc.

Published by Oxford University Press, Inc.
198 Madison Avenue, New York, New York 10016

Oxford is a registered trademark of Oxford University Press

Library of Congress Cataloging-in-Publication Data
Porterfield, Amanda, 1947–
The power of religion: a comparative introduction /
Amanda Porterfield
p.   cm.
ISBN 0-19-509329-1 (pbk.: alk. paper)
1. United States—Religion. I. Title.
BL2525.P668 1997   97-8612
291—dc21   CIP

1 3 5 7 9 8 6 4 2

Printed in the United States of America
on acid-free paper

for Nick

Contents

—ᶆ—

PHOTO GALLERY FOLLOWS PAGE 100

Introduction

This book is an introductory, comparative study of six religious traditions—Native American religions, Christianity,
Judaism, Islam, Hinduism, and Buddhism. The purpose of the
book is to acquaint readers with these traditions, and to stimulate discussion about some of their similarities and differences. In light of the extraordinary increase in religious
diversity in the United States since the 1960s, and in light of
the fact that the United States is now home to virtually every
living religion in the world, the book approaches the religions
of the world through the window of their presence in the
United States today. Based on the assumption that some
understanding of religion and its effects on society is necessary for understanding the world today, the book is intended
for college students as part of their general education, and for
all who are interested in developing their ability to understand
the religious traditions of their neighbors.

The central and organizing theme of the book is the power of
religion. The book focuses on the effects of religion in people's

lives. It explores beliefs as they are lived out in practice and experience. It also explores the roles that religious communities play in shaping religious practice and experience, and the impact of these communities in the larger societies they inhabit.

Many of the book's chapters begin with a religious scene that readers might read about in a newspaper, hear about from a friend or relative, or be directly exposed to, drawn into, or invited to participate in — a Passover seder, a conversation with a Muslim woman wearing a *hajib*, or a visit to a Native American center. The purpose of these descriptions is to convey a sense of what particular religious practices and experiences are like, and how they actually work in people's lives. Historical information and other forms of background material necessary for understanding the events described are included in each chapter, and in the final section of the book on religious community.

The book is divided into three parts — the first on Practice, the second on Experience, the third on Community — each representing one of the main ways that religious beliefs are expressed and make an impact on human life. The first part shows how religious practices can exert a powerful hold on people, and become focal points of people's lives, because they facilitate experiences of divine or ultimate reality. In other words, religious practices are powerful because they are vehicles for religious experience. The second part analyzes several different forms of religious experience and shows how they not only involve people in intense and highly desired relationships with divine or ultimate reality, but also generate loyalty to religious communities and guide people in managing their social world. Thus while religious experiences are intensely personal events that put people in touch with what they understand to be sacred and extraordinary, their power is often manifest in a person's loyalty to a religious community, interactions with other people, and concern for society. The third part explores the impact of religious communities on society in light of increasing religious diversity, especially in the United States. This part also considers some of the ways in which religious practices and experiences are socially constructed.

Parts I and II contain six chapters each. Each part takes up, in turn, each of the six major religious traditions. Thus the chapters in Part I consider, in turn, Navajo sandpainting, the Roman Catholic Eucharist, a Jewish Passover seder, Islamic prayer, Hindu devotional worship, and Zen Buddhist meditation. Part II considers religious experience in each of the six traditions, this time focusing on branches of the traditions different from those considered in the first part. The chapters in Part II discuss Lakota self-sacrifice, Presbyterian grace, Jewish mysticism, Islamic experience of struggling against sin and for God, Hindu experience of the universal body of God, and Tibetan Buddhist awareness of enlightened beings. While none of the chapters exhausts discussion of religious practice or experience in any tradition, each illustrates the transformative power of religion in people's lives.

Each time a new practice or experience is introduced, it provides a point of departure for comparative discussion of some of the practices and experiences already considered within that part. Thus in the part on practice, the Passover seder provides a point of departure for comparative discussion of Navajo sandpainting and the Catholic Eucharist, and discussion of Zen Buddhist meditation offers a framework for comparing all six practices discussed in Part I. These comparisons are designed to be suggestive, to provoke reflection, and to offer starting points for discussion.

The third part on community has a different format. It reviews the main themes of the first two parts, focusing on the way religious practice and experience express belief and define community. Then it takes up the question of the relationship between religious communities and the societies they inhabit, arguing that while the inner workings of religious community have remained pretty much the same over the centuries, the relationship between religious communities and the societies they inhabit has changed considerably. This part looks at society's growing independence from religious control, and at the role that religious diversity plays in this independence. Focusing especially on the United States, this part considers the causes and effects of religious diversity, which has increased dramatically in the United States in recent decades. Religion no longer exerts any overarching control over society in the United States, but religious communities play crucial roles in creating and maintaining the fabric of society through their contributions to individual development, interpersonal relationships, social service, and social trust.

While emphasizing contemporary American religious life, the scope of the book is not limited to the United States today. Each of the chapters and parts of the book attends to the historical and international contexts of current religious events and practices. The chapters on Native American religions emphasize the role that religion has played in enabling Native cultures to survive centuries of European and American colonization. The chapters on Judaism emphasize the long history of Jewish commitment to observing the Torah as well as the international aspect of American Judaism, and especially its relationship to religious and political events taking place in the state of Israel. The chapters on Christianity call attention to the Christian tradition of missionary outreach, and to the international and ethnic diversity of this largest of all religions. The chapters on Islam stress the concept of Islam as a way of life, which contributes to its power as the fastest-growing religion in the United States, and also points to its long history of racial and ethnic inclusiveness, which sets it apart, in the minds of many U.S. converts, from the discrimination against African Americans that has characterized some forms of American Christianity. The chapters on Hinduism place this religion's appeal in the United States today in relation to its development over the course of more than forty centuries in India. And the chapters on Buddhism set its development in the United States in context of numerous strategies for attaining enlightenment handed down over the centuries by Buddhist masters in various parts of the world.

As an introduction to the religions of the world, this book aims to give readers a sense of the flavor and vitality of each tradition. It can stand alone as a basis for thought and discussion, or be used in conjunction with other texts. In whatever way it fits into the reader's interest in religion or program of study, the book is a point of departure for consideration of the power of religion in the lives of individuals, and of its power in the life and development of society today.

THE
POWER
OF
RELIGION

Part I

—⚭—

Religious Practice

Religious practices are repeatable activities that embody the beliefs of a religious community. Through religious practice, people become engaged in religious life, and learn to experience what is ultimate, divine, or sacred for them, both as individuals and as members of a religious group.

In this section, we are using the term practice to include the formal rituals and official ceremonies of religious life, as well as the more personalized, private, and routine activities of daily worship, prayer, and meditation. It is important to note that members of several different religious groups use the term practice more narrowly, and draw an important distinction between practice and ritual. According to this distinction, ritual is associated with formal ceremonies conducted by priestly officials, while religious practice refers more to the discipline of religious activity carried on each day by individuals, families, and communities. In this way of thinking, the term ritual is open to negative connotation as a mere formality that does not always engage the hearts of believers, or facilitate their experience of ultimate, sacred, or divine reality.

For example, many Jews distinguish ceremonial rites, like blowing the *shofar*, or traditional ram's horn, on the Jewish New Year, from the practice of Judaism, which involves the incorporation of Jewish law into daily life. Within Judaism, the distinction between performing the ritual and living the Torah dates back to the destruction of Judaism's cultic center, where ritual sacrifices and other forms of priestly activity had been performed. In response to this event, Jewish *rabbis*, or learned teachers, emphasized God's hidden presence within the everyday world, and the responsibility that all Jews now had to fulfill their partnership with God. The Destruction of the Temple

3

marked the eclipse of ritual control by priestly specialists, and came to be interpreted as a mandate from God for all Jews to take responsibility for the religious order of the world.

Zen Buddhism incorporates a comparable distinction between the performance of formal rites and the practice of meditation. Thus Zen monks are trained to officiate at funerals and at memorial services honoring the life and death of the Buddha Shakyamuni, and they often wear elaborate ceremonial garb to conduct these performances. There are many other ritual acts, like bowing before a statue of a Buddha, that all believers may perform. But none of these ritual acts leads to enlightenment, as does the practice of meditation. The Zen distinction between ritual formalities and the disciplined practice of meditation is expressed in the story of the Zen master who burned a wooden statue of the Buddha in order to stay warm enough to concentrate on his meditation. Not all forms of Buddhism are so deliberately outrageous in their willingness to overthrow ritual custom in order to express the importance of religious practice.

In the broad use of the term applied here, both meditation and formal bows of respect to images of the Buddha qualify as religious practices. Similarly, both living the Torah in everyday family life and blowing the shofar on the Jewish New Year count as religious practices. All of these religious activities embody religious belief. And it is through such active embodiments of belief that people attain experiences of the sacred that impact their lives in powerful ways.

1

Navajo Sandpainting

In small round buildings, or *hogans*, Navajo singers invoke the powers of the *Holy People*, the immortal beings with whom the human people, the *Diné*, share the sacred space of Navajoland. Located in northeast Arizona, and adjacent parts of New Mexico, Utah, and Colorado, Navajoland is a place of changing winds and subtly colored canyons, escarpments, and buttes. The Diné see the physical geography of Navajoland as the outward manifestation of the activities of the Holy People, and they conceptualize the Holy People as the inner forms of the mountains, winds, rains, animals, and other natural phenomena. The Diné attempt to influence the personified forces working within their environment with the help of singers trained to draw strength and goodness from the Holy People, and to subdue or dissipate their malevolent power. Holy People fall into different classes with regard to their relationship to human beings. Some are persuadable, others are not. Some are helpers and intermediaries between human beings and other Holy People, others are undependable or persistently dangerous.

By means of ceremonies, also known in English as *sings* or *chants*, singers attempt to control the Holy People in ways that are therapeutic for human beings. Navajo ceremonies are extremely complex both philosophically and technically, and scholars who have spent years studying them often admit that much eludes them. But some general observations can be made. Particular situations, including potentially propitious events such as weddings and house blessings, as well as unfortunate events such as injuries and disease, prompt the need for ceremonies. Ceremonies are elaborate events often lasting several days and requiring accurate execution. But no organized priesthood exists to prescribe them. Rather, the families of individuals suffering some misfortune, or undergoing an important transition, identify the kind of chant appropriate to the problem at hand, often in consultation with individuals known for their abilities to make such diagnoses, and contract with a singer who specializes in the performance of the particular chant that is required. Of the numerous chants that exist among the Navajo, there are three main types: *Blessingway* chants that prevent disease and other misfortune by drawing in the blessings, or good will, of Holy People; *Holyway* chants that neutralize the potential malevolence of Holy People and transform it into beneficial power; and *Evilway* chants that exorcize Holy People in situations where their malevolence has erupted.

Evilway chants rarely include sandpaintings, since sandpaintings are used to attract the energies of Holy People, and Evilway chants concentrate on dispelling their malevolence. Some Blessingway chants include sandpaintings, although they resemble Pueblo paintings in their small size and utilization of brightly colored vegetable matter. All Holyway chants include sandpaintings that are distinctively Navajo in their design and utilization of dry pulverized materials from charcoal, flower petals, corn meal, pollens, and various kinds of stone.

Holyway chants are actually collections of individual ceremonies divided into two main parts. Each Holyway chant actually begins with ceremonies aimed at dissipating the malevolent potential of the Holy People. These preliminary cleansing ceremonies are followed by ceremonies aimed at attracting the Holy People's goodness and strength, and sandpaintings are part of these ceremonies of attraction. To receive the sun's blessing, Holyway paintings are made during the day, while the chant itself is performed at night. During a two-night Holyway sing, chants focused on sandpainting occur the second night; during a five- or nine-night sing, these chants occur the last four nights, each time over a different painting.

Constructed on the floor of a ceremonial hogan covered smoothly with river sand, Holyway sandpaintings depict one or more Holy People, and range in size from one to twelve square feet and average about six square feet. While a big, elaborate painting can require as much as four hundred hours of work, the average-sized painting takes four or five men about four hours to complete. Beginning at the center and working outward, and using strings held taut to make straight lines, men sift the dried materials between thumb and forefinger to reproduce one of the designs known to the singer, who supervises the work. While hundreds of different designs are known, each singer specializes only in a few. The execution of these designs must be perfect; errors are dangerous and invite malevolence. If a worker makes a mistake, he covers the spot with river sand, and starts again.

During a sandpainting ceremony, the individual for whom the chant is held may sit in the middle of the painting. As the singer calls forth the powers of the Holy People represented in the painting, he applies parts of the painting to various parts of the body of the one-sung-over, with the intention of facilitating a transfer of power between the Holy People and the patient. Anthropologist Gladys A. Reichard described sandpaintings as "ceremonial membranes" through which a kind of "spiritual osmosis" occurs. The Holy People draw evil out of the one-sung-over through the painting, and then infuse him or her with strength and goodness.

The singer's chant guides and controls these activities. In sandpainting as in all Navajo ceremonies, chanting is the chief means by which human beings compel Holy People to serve human well-being. In one of the stories explaining the origin and significance of chanting, First Man and First Woman learned chanting from Wind at the beginning of creation. This ceremonial language became a source of leadership for First Man and First Woman, enabling them and other Holy People, some of whom were progenitors of human clans, to become increasingly self-controlled and work their way through four underworlds into this present fifth world.

In addition to his association with language, Wind made breathing possible and also created the material world through his multicolored components, which are the same winds that blow today in Navajoland. At the beginning of creation a white wind or mist arose from the east and then a blue mist-wind arose from the south. Yellow came from the west at the end of the day, followed by black from the north. These wind-mists lay beautifully on top of each other and from them life was created. But this productive harmony has been disturbed by rituals that give the dark wind a different place. After the birth of First Man and First Woman's two children, who were creatures of incest and hence personifications of inharmonious activity, witches have disturbed the beauty of life. Witches often perform their evil by means of reversing the elements of ceremonial speech.

In the multileveled world of the Navajo, elements at different levels of reality can represent and interact with each other; thus wind nurtures the development of language, while language can invert the natural harmonies of wind. Moreover, events that took place at the beginning of creation coalesce with present events. Thus ceremonies performed today recapitulate the work of creation, and work to restore the original harmonies of the environment established at the time of creation. This artful coalescence is exemplified by two recurrent elements in many chants—*Sa'ah Naaghaii* and *Bik'eh Hozho*— which together mean "long life according to beauty." *Sa'ah Naaghaii* (long life) and *Bik'eh Hozho* (along the path of *hozho*, or harmony and beauty) represent the ideal each Navajo aspires to achieve, the balanced interplay of forces in the environment, the creative efforts of First Boy and First Girl at the time of creation, and the paired forces of thought and speech, which control both individual lives and environmental forces.

In sandpainting ceremonies, this coalescence of multiple dimensions of reality takes place through the singer's chant. The chant brings the painting to life by drawing the Holy People into it, and guides the process of purification and empowerment that occurs in the mind and body of the one-sung-over. By invoking the Holy People, the sandpainting chant leads them to act in ways that will be beneficial to human beings, and defines their agency in terms of the spirit forces within the environment whose activities today replicate the creation of Navajoland. Thus the sandpainting ceremony links the ceremonial treatment of the one-sung-over to the creative energies that first established the world.

Healing is the main purpose of much that goes on in Navajo religious life, and the ceremonies that invoke the creative powers of the environment have real therapeutic effect. As is the case with many systems of religious belief, the ideas involved in Navajo ceremonies offer intellectual explanations that combat feelings of helplessness, anxiety, and fear. But while rituals in many religions impart strength to people by defining relationships between them and powerful forces, the religious practices of Native American and other indigenous groups often identify these forces with aspects of the natural environment. Like many Native religions, Navajo ceremonies facilitate well-being and cause people to feel infused with strength and goodness by fostering a sense of attunement with powerful natural forces.

While healing is an important component of many Native religions, its all-encompassing role in Navajo ceremonial life distinguishes Navajo religion from other Native religions in which individual healing and efforts to guide environmental forces are both important, but not so closely linked to each other as they are in Navajo religion. While invocation of the spirits working within environmental forces is an essential part

of healing ceremonies in virtually all Native religions, including the Navajo religion, the latter is unusual in its focus on
individual healing as the principal means of regulating the
environment and reinstating its original harmony.

Like practitioners of other Native religions, the Navajo
visualize the spirits working with their environment, and call
on those spirits to effect well-being. This process of visualizing
and interacting with the spirits occurs through prayers, songs,
and other forms of religious ceremony that give participants a
sense of involvement in the inner workings of the world and
of contributing to their positive outcome. As a result of this
sense of effective engagement in the world, these religious
practices have an energizing, even transformative, effect on
people's lives.

While the process of engagement with spirits working within
the environment is characteristic of virtually all indigenous religions, the Navajo conceptualization of how the spirit forces in
the environment work together is as distinctive as the Navajo
focus on the cosmic importance of individual healing. In their
outlook on reality, the Navajo conceptualize every aspect of the
world as being constantly in motion. Thus, the harmony of the
world is not a static thing, but a matter of continuous interaction and dynamic balance. This ongoing cosmic balance
involves the participation of human beings and requires their
constant attention. To maintain the beauty and harmony of the
world, every human act, including every sentence spoken,
should involve some recognition of surrounding forces and
attention to their proper relationships and interactions.

Recognition of this interdependence between human
beings and surrounding forces is built into the grammatical
structure of the Navajo language. The verb "to go" is as central
to the construction of Navajo language as the verb "to be" is in
English, and open to even more differentiation; anthropologist Gary Witherspoon counted hundreds of different forms of
"to go" in Navajo. Literally everything that can be spoken of
involves some kind of action, and interaction with other things,
however slow of pace; nothing is inert, or without involvement

with other things. Since accurate information and communication involve some awareness of these interactions, the grammatical construction of Navajo language carries information about which things initiate or dominate motion. Thus nouns representing objects with relatively great force of activity must precede nouns representing objects of lesser activity. As Witherspoon shows, it is customary to say the Navajo equivalent of "the girl drank the water." But it would provoke laughter to say "the water was drunk by the girl," since that way of putting the matter focuses the listener on the activity of the water as it is being drunk by the girl, and conjures up an image of a body of water that is more active and powerful than she going into the girl's mouth.

Navajo ceremonies raise this underlying attentiveness to interaction to the level of deliberate and formalized religious expression. Their concentration on the natural processes of life, and their effort to establish control over these processes through thought and speech, is important for understanding the history of the Navajo people, and for understanding the crucial role that ceremonies have played in enabling the Navajo people to survive, and even flourish, during centuries of domination by other cultures. By fostering commitment to the coalescing processes of change and renewal, and by visualizing these processes as patterns deliberately guided by thought and speech, Navajo ceremonies have figured importantly in the ability of the Navajo people to rebound from a state of defeat and utter poverty in the 1860s to become the largest Indian tribe in the United States and one whose religious traditions are among the most securely intact.

In 1863, as part of plans to subdue the Navajo and fund the Civil War by obtaining the gold and other precious metals erroneously believed to exist in Navajoland, the U.S. Army destroyed the hogans and sheep of Navajoland, and captured eight thousand Navajo men, women, and children, marched them across New Mexico on rations of rancid bacon and weevily flour, and imprisoned them for four years without buildings or tents. During these years of forced removal from their beloved homeland, the Navajo lived without their gods. When finally allowed to return to Navajoland, the survivors reestablished their culture through the traditional ceremonies aimed at recreating therapeutic relationships with the Holy People. These ceremonies not only enabled the Navajo to identify with the strength and beauty of their homeland, but also to associate the processes of change forced on them by western immigrants and U.S. agents with their own traditional respect for movement, and hence with their own healing and empowerment. While religious traditions in other Native groups have sometimes become wedded to images of the past, the Navajo investment in process has facilitated an embrace of social change that is a hallmark of Navajo history. Although on the surface it might seem paradoxical, the acceptance of change, along with a deeply entrenched and constant concern for healing and renewal, has enabled Navajo culture to emerge in the twentieth century as one of the most well-ensconced of Native American cultures.

This willingness to accommodate novelty and change as part of the processes that renew and revitalize the original harmonies of the world has deep roots in Navajo history. Long before the arrival of Euro-Americans, Navajo culture took shape as the nomadic clans of Navajo ancestors appropriated sandpainting and many other elements of belief and life-style from the more highly developed, self-controlled, and sedentary Pueblo cultures of the Southwest. With the arrival of the Spanish in the sixteenth century, the Navajo again altered their life-style dramatically by becoming shepherds who developed weaving as a characteristic cultural expression, and horseback riders who developed trading skills and retained mobility even as sheepherding tied them to particular locales. While elements of both Navajo weaving and sandpainting reflect borrowings from other cultures, these arts have become central to Navajo culture, and scholars agree that the Navajo have developed both of them in highly distinctive ways.

In the twentieth century, the Navajo have displayed considerable success in surviving as a religious subculture amidst the dominating cash economy and consumerist mentality of American culture. The Navajo were among the first, and continue to be among the most successful, in developing tribal artistry as a profitable economic venture, crafting high-quality jewelry and rugs for customers who live outside of Navajoland. This enterprise has contributed to both the economic and cultural strength of Navajo society.

Since the 1930s, a number of Navajo artists have developed new forms of sandpainting specifically designed for commercial market. This development has generated controversy among some conservatives who resist the erosion of religious tradition, and who fear the intrusion of malevolent forces that might be drawn into sandpaintings not controlled by proper ritual. Ceremonial paintings are never fixed to a surface or allowed to remain intact overnight as commercial paintings are, and the remnants of a ceremonial painting that remain after a sing are carefully buried, either at the base of a tree that has been struck by lightning, or some other spot deemed to be safe.

But proponents of commercial sandpainting emphasize the difference between commercial art and the sacred paintings from which it derives. The designs of some commercial paintings may resemble ceremonial ones, but care is often taken to avoid exact duplications that would attract malevolent Holy People. Oftentimes, the designs of commercial paintings depart dramatically from ceremonial art, and the absence of any need for religious sanction in commercial art permits new forms of Navajo creativity. For example, while ceremonial sandpainting is closed to women, commercial sandpainting is open to them, and some women have emerged as artists through this new art form.

The commercial development of sandpainting has helped create a partly secularized domain within a culture otherwise saturated with religious belief and ritual. Interestingly, this secularization process has actually created a cultural space for new forms of religious expression. Commercial sandpaintings have incorporated Christian themes, including at least one painting in which a realistically drawn head of Jesus occupies the central place a Holy Person might occupy in a more traditional painting. More frequent and perhaps more significant are numerous new ways of depicting the beauty of Navajoland. Many commercial paintings portray the sacred space of Navajoland, although not in the same ritually prescribed ways as traditional sandpainting. If they do not carry the same kind of therapeutic power as ceremonial art, commercial renderings engage Navajo artists in the process of communicating important aspects of their culture to outsiders, and thereby help establish widespread recognition of the beauty of Navajoland and its status as a sacred place.

SUGGESTIONS FOR FURTHER READING

Sam Gill, "Whirling Logs and Colored Sands," *Native American Traditions: Sources and Interpretations* (Belmont: Wadsworth Publishing Company, 1983; orig. article 1979).

Raymond Friday Lock, *The Book of the Navajo* (Los Angeles: Mankind Publishing Company, 1992; orig. 1976).

James Kale McNeley, *Holy Wind in Navajo Philosophy* (Tucson: University of Arizona Press, 1981).

Nancy J. Parezo, *Navajo Sandpainting: From Religious Act to Commercial Art* (Albuquerque: University of New Mexico Press, 1991; orig. 1983).

Gladys A. Reichard, *Navajo Religion: A Study of Symbolism* (Princeton: Princeton University Press, 1974; orig. 2 vol. ed. 1950).

Gary Witherspoon, *Language and Art in the Navajo Universe* (Ann Arbor: University of Michigan Press, 1977).

Paul G. Zolbrod, *Diné Bahane: The Navajo Creation Story* (Albuquerque: University of New Mexico Press, 1989; orig. 1984).

2

The Roman Catholic Eucharist

Early one Saturday morning on a New England college campus, a student-athlete preparing for a game later that day joins a small group of worshipers for early *mass*, a set of prayers and ceremonies centering on the *Eucharist*, the Christian practice of receiving bread and wine as the body and blood of Christ. The Eucharist is the central *sacrament*, or religious rite, of the Roman Catholic Church. Like the other six sacraments offered by the Church (baptism, confirmation, marriage, holy orders, penance, and anointing the sick), the Eucharist is a manifestation of the presence of God in the world.

Starting quarterback Derrick Williams came to mass to settle down, to put the game in a good perspective, and to draw on that connection with God's presence celebrated in the Eucharist that, in other moments of his life, had made him feel most completely alive, and most fully attuned to himself and others. His voice joins with others in prayers that acknowledge the forgiving power of God's Holy Spirit, and humanity's need to emulate Christ's obedience to God. These prayers evoke in Derrick a sense of the sacred meaning of life, and a sense of his own responsibility to treat life as a gift from God.

The Eucharist is a ceremony of thanksgiving, with roots in the Jewish ceremonial meal of Passover, which Jesus is believed to have celebrated the night before his death. According to Christian belief, Jesus rose from the dead three days after he was crucified. Since the earliest formation of the Christian Church, believers celebrated this resurrection event with a reenactment of the Last Supper in which bread and wine represented the body and blood of their crucified and risen Lord. As a Christian ceremony, the Eucharist centers on thanksgiving for the *incarnation,* or personification of God in Jesus Christ. As God incarnate in flesh and blood, Christ allowed himself to be sacrificed in order that others might witness and be transformed by his love for humanity and willingness to die for their *sins,* or offenses against God and estrangement from him. For Christians, the Eucharist calls attention to the grand event of Christ's sacrifice, and its power to cleanse the souls of believers, save them from sin, and unite them with God.

In the Catholic Church, believers understand the Eucharist to involve the actual transformation of bread and wine into the body and blood of Christ. Catholics explain this transformation as a *transubstantiation,* or change in the substance of the bread and wine. The doctrine of transubstantiation was described in some detail in the *Summa Theologica* written by the thirteenth-century Dominican friar Thomas Aquinas, who introduced the ideas of the fourth-century Greek philosopher Aristotle into Christianity. The doctrine hinges on the Aristotelian distinction between the "accidents," or external properties of an object that can be perceived by the senses, and the underlying substance that is the essence of the object. In the Catholic doctrine of transubstantiation, the accidents of bread and wine remain after their substance has been changed into the body and blood of Christ. In the sixteenth-century, in response to disagreements over Christian doctrine and practice expressed by Protestants, the Catholic Church made acceptance of transubstantiation a requirement of all believers.

In their Profession of Faith, Catholics assert "that in the most Holy Eucharist there are truly, really and substantially the body and blood, together with the soul and divinity of our Lord Jesus Christ, and that a conversion is made of the whole substance of bread into his body and of the whole substance of wine into his blood, which conversion the Catholic Church calls transubstantiation."

Many practicing Catholics are unconcerned about the precise philosophical meaning of transubstantiation. Some reject the Aristotelian distinction between substance and accidents, maintaining that there is no real substance of bread separable from its physical properties, and emphasizing instead the symbolic expression of Christ's presence in the Eucharist, its powerful impact on the subjective experience of participants, and its importance for the life and work of the church. But whether they interpret transubstantiation literally or symbolically, Catholics would agree that the Eucharist evokes and celebrates the living presence of Christ.

As Derrick watches the gestures and hears the words of the priest bringing forth the body and blood of Christ from bread and wine, he senses the presence of Christ before him on the table that is both the altar of Christ's sacrifice and the table of the fellowship meal that unites his followers. At the culminating moment, as the priest speaks in the person of Christ, saying, "take and eat, this is my body," Derrick feels that the eternal mystery of God is alive and real. Rising and following others to the altar rail, he approaches the priest's assistants, who give him a wafer of bread, saying "the body of Christ," and a cup of wine, saying "the blood of Christ." As the wafer softens and dissolves on his tongue, and the pungent taste of the wine fills his mouth, Derrick feels cleansed and united with God. He returns to his seat with a calm but intense feeling of gratitude and joy.

The Eucharist gives Derrick a sense of *atonement,* or reconciliation with God, that makes him feel at-one with God, himself, and others. The actual tasting and swallowing of the eucharistic elements not only gives him a sense of participation in the body of Christ, but also brings to mind some of the moral cautions about his own body that he has learned from his parents and religious teachers. Used wrongly, he knew, his body could become an expression of sin. When he did sin, Derrick hoped that God would forgive him; he knew that almost any sin could be forgiven through the power of God's love revealed in Christ. But on the football field this afternoon, Derrick would try not to sin, do his best to obey all the rules of the game, keep his self-control, and support his fellow team members, including that second-string quarterback who wanted to outshine him and take his place in the starting lineup.

The focus on Christ's body in the Eucharist also led Derrick to think about the pain he might experience this afternoon. Last Saturday the quarterback on the opposing team had a shoulder dislocated when he was sacked by two of Derrick's teammates. Derrick prayed to the *Virgin Mary*, the saintly Mother of Christ, asking her to keep him from being hurt this afternoon, promising to work harder at his studies if he finished the game unscathed. But if he did get hurt, he prayed that the Holy Mother would help him be brave. He also prayed for the soul of his grandfather, who died last spring. He prayed that his younger brother would do better in school, and asked Mary to help his mother, who was a single parent with a demanding full-time job.

Across the chapel aisle from Derrick was a woman who had just returned to the United States after several months' work with refugees in Africa. She was vowed to poverty, chastity, and obedience as a member of a community of sisters, or religious women. When she had been a student a decade ago, Sister Margaret Parker had spent hours here in the college chapel praying about her *vocation,* or call to religious life. New vocations among young American women were rare in those days, and many communities of Catholic sisters are still declining in size. But Margaret had been raised in a family that was devoted to the church and its teachings, and she wanted a life in which she could completely commit herself to God.

Participating in the mass on a visit back to the college this day, her thoughts are different in many respects from Derrick's, but similar in their orientation to the presence of Christ's body and blood in the Eucharist, and to the power of God's loving spirit in the world. As she joins in the response to the priest's call for repentance and commitment to Christ, Margaret thinks of the anger and unchristian pride she felt as a result of being sent home to the United States rather than being promoted to a position of greater responsibility by the priest supervising her refugee work. She starts to make a mental list of her own failings in her unhappy relationship with the American priest in Africa, and asks God to forgive her impatience and pride. If she had been a more liberal and perhaps less obedient nun, she would also have asked God to strengthen her in the face of the priest's resentment of her popularity, organizational skills, and gender.

Here in the college chapel, as Father Angeli raises the *Host*, the consecrated bread, to show the living presence of God, Margaret is struck by how much easier her relationship is with this priest, and how grateful she is for the careful advice he gave her when she was a student. Father Angeli had helped her untangle her desire to be free of the materialistic American culture she despised from her desire to serve God and devote her life to the sufferings of her fellow human beings. He helped her see that she couldn't begin to serve God until she learned to forgive and love the people around her. Father Angeli had also shown her something about the meaning of religious celibacy, to which he had long been vowed, and which she had more recently undertaken. By watching the commitment he gave to students at the college, Margaret learned that celibacy brought freedom to become engaged in the lives and well-being of others, as well as opportunities to exercise self-sacrifice through relinquishment of conventional marriage and family life, and to become a bride of Christ.

As she receives the body and blood of Christ from Father Angeli at the altar rail, Margaret feels suddenly moved by the immensity of the implications of Christ's sacrifice. She thinks about the children she has worked with in refugee camps, many of them malnourished and diseased, many of them grieving the death of their parents or siblings. In the eyes and in the bodies of these children, Margaret saw the suffering humanity to which God called attention through the sacrifice of his Son and through the manifestation of that sacrifice in the Eucharist. Margaret is drawn to these children with all her heart; she has seen Christ in their eyes and in their bodies. She believes that the redemption of the world lies in them, and in loving them and other children around the world. She feels a renewed sense of gratitude to have been called to serve them, and a renewed sense of hope that God will open another way for her to serve them.

Through their participation in the mass, both Derrick and Margaret experience a sense of purification and closeness to God that sends them back into their lives with energy, commitment, and emotional balance. In these important respects, the effect of the Eucharist is similar to the effect of Navajo sandpainting ceremonies. In both cases, the recipients of the spiritual power conveyed through the ceremonies feel cleansed, strengthened, and attuned to the world. The underlying operation of the two ceremonies is also similar. In both the transubstantiation of bread and wine into the body and blood of Christ and in the penetration of Holy People into the ceremonial membrane of a Navajo sandpainting, participants feel a powerful divine presence passing through a ritually constructed material form. The ritual process through which recipients come to feel infused with a divine presence can also be compared. The Catholic priest gives members of his congregation bits of the consecrated elements to eat and drink, and the Navajo singer transposes parts of the sandpainting onto the body of the one-sung-over. In both cases, material ingredients transmitted to the recipient's body serve as a vehicle for transmitting the spiritual power of a divine being.

The two ceremonies are also characterized by an underlying similarity in the relationship between spirit and matter, which might be described as reverence for the embodiment

of spiritual power in the material world. Thus the Roman
Catholic focus on the incarnation of God, and strong belief
in the visible and sensual signs of God's presence in the
world, is similar to the Navajo belief that the spiritual presence of the Holy People is manifest in certain aspects of the
material world. Catholic appreciation of the beauty of natural
life, as seen from the perspective of God's redeeming love, is
also similar to Navajo respect for the beauty of the environment, and to Navajo desire to walk in beauty with the spirits
who have created the world.

Although historically the Roman Catholic Church often
emphasized the tension between spirit and flesh, equated
flesh with sin, and made the denial of flesh an aspect of Christian life, a long tradition of praise for the visible and sensual
signs of God's presence also characterizes Catholic spirituality,
and may help explain the relative ease with which many Native
people have embraced Catholic belief and ritual during the
last five centuries of Native American contact with Catholic
missionaries. Although the Navajo never entered the Roman
Church in large numbers, other Native groups have significant Catholic representation, and some spokespersons for
Native American religions have been Catholic. Thus Nicholas
Black Elk, the well-known Oglala Sioux holy man who died in
1950, was also a Catholic catechist who believed that the collective presence of spirit beings known as *Wakan Tanka* was
coextensive with the Christian God. For Black Elk, Native
American respect for the spirits who revealed themselves in
natural form was compatible with Catholic respect for the
incarnation of God in the living presence of Christ in the
world. This kind of Native-Catholic syncretism has become
increasingly popular in recent years. While elements of Native
art have long been part of Catholic churches with Native
members, some of these churches have taken new steps to
blend Native American and Roman Catholic belief and ritual,
to acknowledge the similar role of suffering and sacrifice in
Native religions and Christianity, and to affirm the respect for
life manifest in Native cultures.

However, several important differences exist between the official teachings of the Roman Catholic Church regarding the incarnation and Navajo ideas about the spiritual activities of Holy People in Navajoland. First, in their concern to maintain relationships with Holy People that promote long life according to beauty, the Navajo avoid death because of its potential to attract malevolent power. As a result, a ceremony focusing so vividly on sacrifice and death, like the Roman Catholic Eucharist, would be abhorrent from a traditional Navajo perspective, and this helps explain why so few Navajo are Catholic. Second, the Navajo recognize malevolent or potentially malevolent Holy People, in some contrast to Catholics, for whom God is entirely good. Evil certainly exists in Catholic thought, and has often been personified as the devil, and in some cases subject to ritual exorcisms not unlike Navajo Evilway ceremonies, but many Catholic theologians have emphasized the idea that evil is the absence of good rather than a distinct power over or against God. Third, while the Navajo recognize numerous Holy People, some closely related and others relatively independent of one another, Roman Catholics believe in no more and no less than one God in three persons—Father, Son, and Holy Spirit. And the relationships among these three-persons-in-one are defined rather specifically—God is the Father and Creator of the world, Christ is the Son of God and God made flesh, and the Holy Spirit is the power of God's love. Fourth, while the Navajo interpret the material world as the manifestation of spiritual powers, official Catholic teaching prohibits the equation of God with the natural forces of the universe. But this Catholic avoidance of pantheism, and insistence that the incarnation be understood exclusively in terms of Christ, his sacraments, and his Church, coexists with respect for the natural world as God's creation, and with the belief that God makes himself known in the world through visible signs. Thus when apprehended through Christ, his sacraments, and his Church, the world becomes a sacred place.

Perceiving the world through the lens of the sacraments gives the world itself a sacramental quality, and can lead to a mystical appreciation of natural beauty. As the Catholic convert Robert Lowell wrote in his poem, "At the Indian Killer's Grave," from *Lord Weary's Castle,*

> Gospel me to the Garden, let me come
> Where Mary twists the warlock with her flowers—
> Her soul a bridal chamber fresh with flowers
> And her whole body an ecstatic womb.

In this poetic vision, a garden is a symbolic landscape and its flowers have a religious meaning that enhances the viewer's appreciation of their beauty. This Catholic way of infusing nature with religious meaning can be contrasted with Protestant disbelief in the redemptive power of the sacraments and with the Protestant tendency to emphasize the disjuncture between nature and grace. As many Protestant theologians have argued, grace breaks into the natural order to transform the human will and overturn its natural inclinations. While Protestant recipients of grace respect and praise the natural world as God's creation, they would be less likely than Catholics to see a garden, or any other natural scene, as a dramatization of Christian grace.

In recent years, some Catholic writers have taken the sacramentalization of nature beyond poetry into the domains of science. On of the first and most well-known of these writers was the Jesuit mystic and paleontologist Pierre Teilhard de Chardin, who interpreted biological evolution as the upward spiraling of the material world toward God. Teilhard urged his readers to see the working out of Christ's incarnation everywhere, even in the most material aspects of the universe. Staunchly devoted to the Catholic Church as the chief expression of and guide into the mystery of God, he identified it as the central pathway of humankind's spiritual evolution.

Followers of such efforts to find God in all things, including the processes of biological evolution and ecological balance, are numerous in the Catholic Church today, especially in the United States. While often distinctly Christian and Catholic, their outlooks on the upreaching, mystical presence of God in the world bears interesting similarities to the Navajo story of creation as a progressive, upward emergence of life forms, consciousness, and social behavior.

Other comparisons between the Eucharist and Navajo ceremonies are also useful, including that of concern for proper procedure. As historians of the Roman Church have noted, insistence on the correct performance of the Eucharist has enabled the church to maintain both the centrality and mystery of that ceremony in Catholic religious life. The elements of the Eucharist must be carefully handled and consumed, and the exact performance of certain gestures and words is essential to the priest's ability to effect transubstantiation. A similar concern for proper procedure is evident in Navajo sandpainting ceremonies, although, unlike the Eucharist, these ceremonies are various, and different paintings and chants are known to different singers. But the prescribed design of each painting must be executed exactly, chants must be sung in proper order, leftover material carefully disposed of, and various precautions taken by the one-sung-over and his or her family.

Concern for rules and procedures also characterizes the behavioral expectations of both Catholics and Navajos. According to Catholic thought, everyone suffers estrangement from God, and everyone stands in need of the atonement provided through Christ's sacrificial love, and through the sacraments he instituted to bring individuals closer to God. Different degrees of sin exist for Catholics — venial sins are personal weaknesses or failures that prevent a person's wholehearted commitment to God, while mortal sins sever a person's relationship to God and lead him or her to hell, unless those sins are absolved. Catholic preoccupation with classifying various forms of sin and penance declined significantly after the Second Vatican Council in the 1960s, when the head of the Roman Catholic Church, and the administrative deputy of Christ on earth, Pope John XXIII, led the church away from legalistic interpretations of Christian life toward a recommitment to

Christ's life-affirming role in the world. Although an upsurge in conservative Catholicism is occurring today among American Catholics, especially among young adults, many Catholics in the United States believe that their church is still too rigid on issues involving sex, especially birth control, and choose not to follow the church's teachings on certain points. But general moral precepts remain firmly in place for most American Catholics, including the idea that compassion for the poor is a hallmark of Christian life, and the belief that social life should be governed by principles of justice and mercy.

Although the concept of sin does not exist in Navajo religion, the Navajo concern to identify problematic relationships with Holy People, and repair those relationships, functions similarly to the Catholic concern to identify and repair estrangement from God. In both Catholic and Navajo life, inappropriate relationships with divine power can play themselves out in social relationships, and believers turn to religious ceremony to repair the relationships with divine power that cause their social relationships to be in disarray. Like many Christians, Catholics not only believe in treating others with respect, but emphasize the importance of seeing Christ in the lives of others, especially in the lives of those who are poor and suffering. Catholics believe that God sees and judges the love they show in these relationships, and they seek forgiveness from God when their love falls short.

In Navajo culture, interpersonal behavior is a subject of moral concern, and carefully regulated. Thus appropriate behaviors are prescribed for various types of kinship relations. For example, the mother of a married woman is expected to behave bashfully toward her daughter's husband, while he is expected to treat her with extreme respect and avoidance. Brothers are expected to interact by joking with one another in patterned ways, and male cross-cousins are also expected to joke with one another, but more strenuously than brothers do.

While social relationships among the Navajo are more ritualized than social relationships for most Catholics in America today, members of certain Catholic religious communities, especially those cloistered from the world, find all aspects of life carefully orchestrated to exhibit worship of God, with daily life revolving around periodic sessions of prayer. Moreover, relationships among members of these Catholic religious communities are defined in terms of spiritual kinship; thus "brothers" live in a monastery, and "sisters" in a convent. Even in ordinary Catholic life, priests are called "Father" and women vowed to religious life are called "Sister."

But while these purely religious relationships differ from the natural kinship ties that characterize Navajo life, for most Catholics, religious life is also deeply intertwined with natural family ties. The Catholic Church sees itself as a guardian of family life and values; marriage is a holy sacrament, divorce is highly problematic in the eyes of the church, and abortion is unacceptable. On a larger social and cultural scale, tribelike ties of ethnicity have also been deeply intertwined with Catholic religious life, especially in the United States, where ethnic groups have relied on Catholic religious life to help establish and maintain the ethnic identification of group members. Thus in late-nineteenth and early-twentieth-century America, Catholic enclaves in Boston, New York, Chicago, and other cities were often divided along ethnic lines, with Irish Catholics typically dominating other groups. Even today in a few Catholic churches in the United States, the altar is carpeted in bright green, a symbol of Irish soil and of the fusion of ethnic and religious allegiance that characterizes parish leaders. Among Italian American Catholics after World War I, Catholic religious life was not only interwoven with Italian culture and family life, but also with Italian nationalism, as Italian priests helped emigrants from different parts of Italy forge bonds with one another in the United States through identification with the ideology of national socialism promoted by Italy's Fascist party. In each of these cases, the fusion of Catholic religious life with a particular ethnic culture helped members of religious and ethnic minorities defend, define, and advance themselves.

But however intense the ties between Catholicism and particular ethnic cultures, these ties have always existed in some tension with the concept of the Roman Catholic Church as a universal church. Because the church is a centralized, hierarchically structured, and authoritative institution that presides over the training and discipline of the priests who celebrate the Eucharist, Catholics are unified, at least to some degree, by that ceremony and the church it represents. The word *catholic* means universal, and the Eucharist does not belong to any particular culture, but is understood to be both inclusive and transcendent of all cultures. For centuries, all Roman Catholic priests chanted the words of the mass in Latin, and at least in theory, the Eucharist was performed exactly the same way in Catholic communities around the world. After Vatican II, in response to concern that the Latin mass had lost some of its meaning for people in the mid-twentieth-century world and in an effort to make the meaning of the mass more clearly accessible, priests were encouraged to face their congregations while consecrating the elements, and to say the mass in the *vernacular*, or ordinary language of the people. These changes in ceremonial procedure underscore the church's affirmation of diverse cultures, as well as its commitment to the larger concept of the universal body of the church, defined both as the people of God and as the living body of Christ on earth.

In some contrast, Navajo culture is deeply grounded in Navajo religion, and religion distinguishes Navajo culture from other cultures. Thus the Navajo people are defined, to an important extent, by the particular religious rituals they practice. Although this correspondence between the members of Navajo society and the practitioners of Navajo religion is not complete — some Christian Navajo do not participate in traditional ceremonies, and those ceremonies are not completely closed to outsiders — the customs of Navajo society and the ceremonies of Navajo religion are coextensive and mutually reinforcing in many respects. Thus avoidance of disharmony characterizes Navajo relationships with both human kin and Holy People, and Navajo ceremonies express in formal terms the respect for the spiritual forces at work in the environment that is expected in ordinary behavior.

Moreover, these customs and ceremonies are linked quite specifically to a particular geographical place, with the Holy People perceived as inhabiting and expressing themselves through the mountains, winds, rains, and animals of Navajoland. Navajo religion remains tied to a specific locale inhabited by a particular ethnic group whose identity is defined by that locale and its religion. In this respect Navajo religion is significantly different from Catholicism, which emphasizes that the Spirit of God is ubiquitous, and not tied to any particular place. Both Derrick Williams and Sister Margaret Parker can receive the Eucharist anywhere, receive the same comfort and empowerment, and experience the incarnation of God, and the Spirit of his presence, wherever that ceremony takes place.

But here again, it is important not to draw too rigid a distinction between Catholic universalism and Navajo particularism. In popular Catholic devotion, particular geographical sites have been venerated as sacred places, and have often been linked to the veneration of Mary, the saint among saints renowned for her accessibility and willingness to intervene on behalf of those who pray to her. Although in many instances they have flourished without official church sanction, Catholic shrines like those at Lourdes and Medjugorje have drawn millions of pilgrims seeking cures and blessings from waters believed to be sacred or from visions of the Holy Mother received by peasant girls. Such shrines and miracles have long been an important factor in the popularity of Catholic piety, and point again to Catholicism's tendency to religious syncretism, in which beliefs and practices associated with Catholic religious life often become coextensive with beliefs and practices indigenous to particular locales.

This accommodation of popular culture is also reflected in the Catholic veneration of saints. Although Catholic saints are believed to have exemplified the compassion, self-sacrifice, and power of God's love in the course of their human life, the immortal holy people in the Catholic religion function like the Navajo Holy People insofar as Catholics try to obtain blessings, protections, and cures from their saints much as the Navajo try to obtain blessings, protections, and cures from their Holy People. However, while no centralized authority exists among the Navajo to identify Holy People or invest them with spiritual status, the Roman Church has defined the stages through which holy people must pass en route to sanctification, including blessedness or *beatification*, as well as a set of requirements that advocates of a holy person's candidacy for sainthood must meet, such as evidence of that person's conformity to church doctrine, contribution to the faith of others, and ability to perform miracles. But the veneration of saints is also a means by which ordinary people without church office define the contours of their own religious life, and the church's control over this veneration is limited. Praying to Saint Jude for relief from sickness, to Saint Christopher for a safe journey, to the Madonna of Mount Carmel for the soul of one's child, or to the Mary in her shrine at Lourdes are means by which Catholic people make Catholic religious life their own.

In sum, Catholic efforts to obtain the blessings of saints are similar to Navajo efforts to obtain the blessings of Holy People, and the celebration of the incarnation of Christ in the Eucharist is similar, in certain important ways, to the appreciation of the visible beauty of Navajoland fostered in sandpainting ceremonies. The universality of the Eucharist, its focus on the singular drama of Christ's redemptive sacrifice, and the institutional structure supporting it make the Eucharist quite different from Navajo sandpainting. But the worship of personified beings with supernatural power, and the discovery of strength, happiness, and attunement with the world through that worship, makes the two ceremonies comparable.

SUGGESTIONS FOR FURTHER READING

Henry Bettenson, ed., *Documents of the Christian Church*, (London: Oxford University Press, 1963).

Denise L. Carmody and John T. Carmody, *Roman Catholicism: An Introduction* (New York: Macmillan Publishing Company, 1990).

Pierre Teilhard de Chardin, *The Heart of the Matter* (New York: Harcourt Brace Jovanovich, 1978).

Lawrence S. Cunningham, *The Catholic Experience* (New York: Crossroad Press, 1985).

Philip Gleason, *Keeping the Faith: American Catholicism Past and Present* (Notre Dame, Indiana: University of Notre Dame, 1987).

Michael J. Himes and Stephen J. Pope, eds., *Finding God in All Things: Essays in Honor of Michael J. Buckley, S.J.* (New York: Crossroad Publishing Company, 1996).

Robert A. Ludwig, *Reconstructing Catholicism for a New Generation* (New York: Crossroad Publishing Company, 1995).

Robert Anthony Orsi, *The Madonna of 115th Street: Faith and Community in Italian Harlem, 1880-1950* (New Haven: Yale University Press, 1985).

Eduard Schillebeeckx, *Christ* (New York: Seabury Press, 1980).

3

A Jewish
Passover Seder

"This is the bread of slavery which our ancestors ate in Egypt when they were slaves. Let all who are hungry come and eat." As Ben Dorfman, a family doctor, reads these words, he is seated at the dinner table in his Manhattan apartment, surrounded by his wife, mother, three children, and a few family friends. It is Passover, the Jewish holiday celebrating the liberation of the people of Israel from Egypt. Putting down the *Haggadah*, the written narrative telling the story of the Exodus and giving instruction for the organization of the Passover meal, Dr. Dorfman looks around the table and says, "This is the night we remember how God led the Jews out of slavery. On this night, Pharaoh let the Jews go because he was afraid of God. We call it *Pesah* or Passover," Dr. Dorfman went on, turning to his twelve-year-old son, Jake, "because God passed over the houses of Jews when he sent the last of his ten plagues to punish Pharaoh. While all the first-born Egyptian sons were killed in the plague, the Jews marked their homes with the blood of lambs, which they sacrificed to God, and their sons were protected."

Opening his hand toward the plate of flat, unleavened bread, or *matzoh*, near the middle of the table, Dr. Dorfman looks over to his daughter's college roommate, Elizabeth, who has never before been to a meal organized as a *seder*, or ritual progression. "Matzoh symbolizes the hard crusts the Jews ate when they were poor slaves. It also symbolizes the Jews' freedom. When they heard that Pharaoh would let them go, the Jews baked some bread to take with them in their journey out of Egypt. They were in a hurry because they knew Pharaoh might change his mind, so they didn't have time to let the bread rise. It was hard and flat, but it was the most delicious bread they had ever eaten because they were free."

The matzoh and its symbolism are central to Passover — another name for which is *hag ha-matzot*, the holiday of the unleavened bread. Matzoh not only symbolizes the freedom of the Jews, but also the pure and passionate commitment to God with which the Jews embraced their freedom. In contrast to this freedom and commitment to God represented by matzoh, *hametz*, or food containing yeast, symbolizes the dependence and passivity of slavery, and also the evil or impurity lurking within the individual. This impurity may be tolerated during the rest of the year as part of human nature, but at Passover, it must be identified and removed. Many Jews throw away all the hametz in their homes, or seal it in a cabinet, or sell it in preparation for Passover. Stoves, refrigerators, sinks, kitchen cabinets, counters, and any room where crumbs of hametz might have been dropped during the year are cleansed and made *Pesahdik*, or ready for Passover. Children participate in a family ritual of hunting for hametz, searching for crumbs and often discovering larger pieces their parents have hidden for them to find.

As Reform Jews, the Dorfmans do not feel bound to observe every Jewish ritual. Leaving aside certain parts of the preparation for Passover that, in their judgment, do not contribute significantly to their lives, they feel free to celebrate the parts that are most meaningful and important to them. They give their apartment, and especially the kitchen, a good cleaning, but don't rinse the sink and kitchen counters with boiling water, or heat the oven for twenty-four hours, as more observant Jews do. They have a special set of dinner plates for Passover, but not a separate set of pots and pans with which to cook Passover foods as other Jews do. They eat matzoh instead of bread and pasta during Passover week, and at home, they try to bypass other foods that contain yeast—such as vinegar, soda, and dried fruit—but they still go out to restaurants where food containing yeast may be unavoidable. They are simply not as scrupulous as more observant Jews are about the Passover restriction against hametz.

However much the degree of religious observance varies, Passover is the holiday most often celebrated by Jews. By one account, as many as 90 percent of all Jews participate in a Passover seder every year. The popularity of this holiday is directly related to its family appeal and strong connection with home life. Although synagogue congregations hold special services and even special seders for their members and friends, the main event of the Passover holiday is the family seder. The importance and popularity of this event under-scores the strong family orientation built into the structure of Jewish religious practice.

Favorite traditions associated with the Passover seder include the seder plate, which holds several foods that symbolize various aspects of the holiday. A fresh sprig of parsley represents the renewal of life each spring, when Passover always occurs, and the spiritual renewal symbolized by that season. During the seder, one of the participants dips the parsley in salt water to remember the tears the Jews shed as slaves. Horseradish also represents the bitterness of slavery, and participants dip this herb in *haroset*, a mixture of apples, nuts, wine, and spices. Haroset symbolizes the mortar the Jews used in making bricks when they were slaves and also the sweet hope of freedom. A roasted egg represents the sacrifice offered by Jews in the temple in Jerusalem, and a roasted bone the sacrifice of the lambs in Egypt.

The Passover table also holds a goblet for Elijah, the prophet who announces the coming of the Messiah. According to legend, Elijah visits every home on Passover, and the wine in the goblet often disappears mysteriously during the seder. At the end of the meal, the youngest child opens the front door to welcome Elijah, and the coming of the Messiah. At the Dorf-man home, eight-year-old Miriam opens the apartment door at the appropriate moment, and glances up and down the hall-way hoping to catch a glimpse of the mysterious stranger.

The popularity of Passover stems not only from its capacity for combining homemade family entertainment with religious instruction, but also from the power of the story reenacted in the seder meal, and the importance of that story for Jewish life. As far as most Jews are concerned, the Exodus story is "The Greatest Story Ever Told." Among the many stories asso-ciated with Jewish tradition, the Exodus story defines Jewish identity most centrally.

The reenactment of this story at Passover occupies a central place in the Jewish ritual calendar, and leads to *Shauvot* seven weeks later, the holiday celebrating the covenant the Jews established with God after escaping from Egypt, and the Ten Commandments Moses received from God at Mount Sinai. The Exodus story also plays a central role in *Sukkot*, the holi-day six months after Passover celebrating the autumn harvest and commemorating the forty-year journey of God's people in the desert after they received the covenant at Sinai. During Sukkot, families and communities construct booths replicat-ing the fragility and openness of desert dwellings. During meals and, in some cases, sleep overs in the booths, the excite-ment of a family camping adventure dovetails with religious images of the joyful comraderie of earlier Jews living simply in the desert, free from bondage and committed to God.

The Exodus story plays a less prominent role at other times of the year, but persists in the background of other holidays as a defining moment in Jewish history, and a defining element of Jewish identity. For example, during Yom Kippur, when Jews focus inwardly on their own mortality and shortcomings, feel-ings of gratitude and responsibility to God for their freedom are inherent in their concern for atonement. Similarly, the

Exodus marks the beginning of Jewish nationhood, whose renewal is celebrated during Hanukkah, the Festival of Lights commemorating the rededication of the Temple in Jerusalem after its recovery from the Greeks in the second century B.C.E. For many Jews in the United States, Hanukkah is an important alternative to Christmas. The distinctiveness of Jewish identity is underscored for many Jews during December, when lavish celebrations more or less related to the birth of Jesus impinge dramatically on everyone's work and school schedules, including those of non-Christians, and on a wide range of social interactions and economic forces. The simultaneity of Hanukkah and Christmas festivities brings home to many Jews the special meaning of the Exodus story for them as a religiously separate people, and the distinctiveness of their own history.

Grounded in the Exodus story, the Jewish ritual calendar marks the progression of time from one season of the year to the next. This calendar also carries within it the fundamental elements of Jewish identity. In the words of Rabbi Irving Greenberg, "The Holy Days are the unbroken master code of Judaism. Decipher them and you will discover the inner sanctum of this religion. Grasp them and you hold the heart of the faith in your hand." For Rabbi Greenberg and many other Jews, the holidays provide important education about various aspects of Jewish faith and major events in Jewish history. At the same time, the holidays mark the high points in the terrain of religious life, which Jews define in terms of the observance of Jewish law.

Through this observance, Jews express their commitment to Jewish law, which is the basis of Jewish religious life. In addition to the Ten Commandments, there are hundreds of prescriptions in the *Torah*, the centerpiece of Jewish law, which in its narrowest definition means the Five Books of Moses — Genesis, Exodus, Leviticus, Numbers, and Deuteronomy. Torah can also refer to all the biblical writings recognized by Jews, including the Psalms, Prophets, and other writings, and in more expansive definitions, to all the interpretations and applications of God's commandments. The first and foremost of these interpretations is the *Mishnah,* a written digest of the oral traditions and rules for observing religious law compiled in the late second or early third century of the common era. *Rabbis,* or learned scholars of religious law, wrote commentaries, called *Talmud,* on the Mishnah and other compilations of religious law. The most influential of these commentaries is the Babylonian Talmud, which was composed in the mid-fifth and sixth centuries of the common era.

The vast expanse of *halakah,* or rules, interpretations, and applications of religious law, continues to be elaborated upon, and governs everything from daily prayers to the regulation of sexual activity. The two aspects of halakah that most commonly distinguish observant Jews in the United States today are the procedures for suspending work on *Shabbat,* the Sabbath, in honor of God, and *kashrut,* the dietary laws that honor God's creation by separating dairy foods, which are naturally produced by animals as part of creation, from meat, which must be killed to be eaten, and therefore must be handled in specially prescribed ways that minimize violence and blood. Through meticulous observance of Shabbat and kashrut, Orthodox Jews set themselves apart from other members of society, including other Jews.

While obedience to Jewish law is the basis of Jewish religion, Jews differ dramatically among themselves in their understanding of which rules they must observe in order to be faithful to God, and in their understanding of how much authority each individual Jew has to interpret the rules. Orthodox Jews are committed to living the Torah and observing halakah in every aspect of life; they place more emphasis than more liberal Jews on the separation between religious life and modern society. This tendency to separatism among Orthodox Jews is driven by the conviction that Jewish life requires ritual observance of the whole fabric of Jewish law. In contrast, more liberal Jews believe that they should not be held responsible for perpetuating cultural practices of a bygone era, and that tradition should have "a vote but not a veto" in determining their behavior. Liberal Jews also stress the contributions that Jewish values can make, and have made, to modern society, emphasizing that the values embedded in the Torah are centered in commitment to justice and truth. Liberal Jews are proud of the many contributions to western civilization that have flowed out of Jewish writings about the importance of justice, and out of the respect for learning that is characteristic of Jewish culture and rooted in love for the Torah.

In actuality, there are many Judaisms, and the absence of any centralized authority or priesthood ensures this heterogeneity. Orthodox Jews attempt to simplify things by regarding other Jews as nonreligious, but Orthodoxy itself is as diverse a phenomenon as any other branch of Judaism. Outside Orthodox circles, many shades of religious difference also exist. Reform Jews define religious life in the context of their full participation in society, and the contributions they can make to compassion and justice in the world. Conservative Jews, as the name suggests, place more emphasis on adherence to halakah than Reform Jews, but separate themselves from the larger society to a far lesser degree than Orthodox Jews, and often emphasize the importance of distinguishing abiding religious principles from prescriptions no longer applicable to modern life.

While commitment to halakah and interpretations of it vary among Jews, belief in the concept of God's law, and in observance of it as the essence of religious life, characterizes all forms of religious Judaism. As the defining element of Jewish religion, the practice of living God's law is often highly individualized and internalized, even in Orthodox circles. As rabbis across the spectrum of Judaism emphasize, religious observance should never be just going through the paces, but is rather meant to be a way of consciously attending to the presence of God in all aspects of life.

In certain respects, this attitude toward the observance of Jewish law is similar to the religious attitude encouraged in the Roman Catholic celebration of the Eucharist described in the preceding chapter. Participation in the Catholic rite of the Eucharist is meant to bring the Christian into an experience of the presence of God, enabling the Christian to behave in a way that is mindful of God. Like the observant Jew, the good Catholic shuns superficial participation in religious observance, but at the same time views religious observance, when devoutly practiced, as the highest form of religious experience.

In addition to this important general similarity between Jewish and Catholic attitudes toward religious observance, there are specific points of continuity between the Catholic Eucharist and the Passover seder. Indeed, the religious and historical roots of the Eucharist can be traced to the Passover seder which, according to Christian tradition, was the Last Supper Jesus and his disciples celebrated the night before he was crucified. But in the Eucharist, the symbolism of the Passover seder is transformed by its identification with Jesus and his identification with God. Jesus himself becomes the lamb sacrificed by the Jews to God, and his body and blood become the bread and wine consumed by believers.

Thus for Christians, the Exodus story is more than an important historical narrative about the founding of the nation of Israel and the special relationship God established with the Jews. It is also a prolegomena to the greater and enfolding story of Christ. Like the Exodus, the suffering, death, and resurrection of Christ is about freedom from bondage. But it is the freedom from bondage to sin that Christians are primarily concerned about, and in their view, Christ offers this freedom to all humankind. Moreover, in the Christian story, the Jews are no longer the principle recipients of divine blessing. From the Christian perspective, God's incarnation in Jesus Christ supersedes his historical relationship with the people of Israel.

In Christian belief, Jesus Christ not only fulfills the law, but also abolishes its hold as a requirement of faith. While they regard the Ten Commandments as God-given rules for human behavior, and their churches provide instruction to guide the behavior of their members, Christians believe that Christ released believers from the punishments they deserve for not being able to obey God's law, and that reliance on his forgiveness and grace is the only way to salvation. Thus the Catholic

Church teaches that the appropriate performance of religious ritual does not revolve around the law of God revealed in the Torah, but rather around participation in the sacraments of the Catholic Church, which disclose the mercy and grace of Christ.

Protestants go a step further in drawing a contrast between the observance of law and the reception of grace. During the last several centuries, Protestants have stressed their dependence on Christ's grace by emphasizing that obedience to God's law cannot be achieved by human effort. They have even interpreted Catholic belief in the power of the sacraments as an example of the investment in ritual observance that Christ overturned. Thus Christians differ among themselves over the exact meaning of the Eucharist, as they do over questions about how grace is linked to good works and the obedience of the Ten Commandments. But they agree in the belief that grace supersedes Jewish law.

From the Jewish perspective, this belief is deeply problematic and responsible, at least in part, for the long history of persecution that Jews have suffered. Offended by their failure to recognize Christ as the Messiah, and by their insistence on ritual observance of the law, Christians have often stereotyped Jews as stubborn and mean-spirited people, and blamed them for the death of Jesus. In some cases, Christians have even questioned the Jews' right to exist. Such attitudes led to the *Holocaust* during World War II, in which Nazis led by Adolf Hitler killed six million Jews in a systematic effort to exterminate the Jewish "race."

Of course, many Christians hold Jews in high esteem, and are proud to count them as neighbors and friends. But even in this friendly context, Jews often play a role in Christian thought that makes Jews uncomfortable. When Christians recast Jewish history and scripture through the prism of Christian belief in Jesus Christ as the incarnate Son of God, the Torah becomes the "Old" Testament, and the stories in this scripture become spiritualized in terms of New Testament revelation. Thus for Christians, Jewish history and Jewish identity are symbolic of something that Jews themselves do not recognize or agree to.

This is not to say that Jews are uncomfortable with spiritualized interpretations of biblical events, or with investing religious objects with symbolic meaning. As we have seen, Jewish
ritual is full of spiritual symbolism, and any ritual object or
action can have multiple symbolic meanings. Thus matzoh
symbolizes at least several things simultaneously — the hard
crusts the Jews ate when they were slaves, the freedom they
enjoyed when released from bondage, and the inner purity
that characterized their ancestors' commitment to God, and
also characterizes their own commitment as it is renewed during the Passover holiday. Rabbinic interpretation of Jewish
law adds layer upon layer of symbolic meaning to the commandments described in the Torah, and observant Jews bring
as many of those layers as they can into their religious practice, making their daily lives a pageant of religious awareness
and praise.

In this respect, the Orthodox Jew is similar to the traditional Navajo discussed in the first chapter of this book. Much
as Jewish law is a blueprint for structuring behavior, Navajo
taboos and ceremonies govern social interaction, engagement
with the natural world, and attitudes toward sexuality, personal identity, and death. Much as the Orthodox Jew experiences the presence and power of God through the practice of
religious law, the traditional Navajo experiences the presence
and powers of the Holy People by avoiding certain proscribed
behaviors and performing ceremonial actions that bring
human beings into closer contact with divine power.

Jewish ritual does not involve the same effort to govern
interactions among spiritual forces. Indeed, Jews explicitly
reject the idea that divine reality is multiple, divided against
itself, or vulnerable to human manipulation. But both Navajo
and Jewish rituals are concerned with enactments of sacred
stories that facilitate religious experience. The Passover seder
reenacts the Exodus story and thereby brings the freedom
given by God a living reality for Jews today. Similarly, Navajo
sandpainting ceremonies reenact particular events in the
Navajo creation story that enable participants to experience

the powers of creation as living realities. As we have seen, Navajo creation stories provide models for understanding the spiritual cause of the illness or misfortune prompting the need for a ceremony, and for restoring the spiritual balance believed to produce health and good fortune. As the ceremonial enactment of these stories brings the forces of creation alive, they can have a powerful therapeutic effect.

While it is more predominant in Navajo ceremony, both Jewish and Navajo rituals are concerned with healing. Ritual observance brings the Jew into relationship with a tradition of religious experience and communal belonging that can salve the wounds of persecution and misunderstanding that Jews have often suffered. Moreover, one of the principal goals of ritual observance is *tikkun olam*, the perfection or reparation of the world. Among Orthodox Jews, this commitment to perfecting the world involves the effort to restore, in their own lives and families, the open relationship that Adam and Eve enjoyed with God in the Garden of Eden before their Fall into disobedience of God's law. Among liberal Jews, the mandate to repair the world involves a commitment to bringing the power of justice, which is central to the stories about God and his people, to bear on the divisiveness and inequality in the larger social world.

Jewish practice also carries a unique historical focus tied to the long history of the Jewish people. Because Jews believe that God reveals himself through history, Jewish practice focuses on historical events in a way that Navajo ritual does not. Thus Jewish holidays reenact landmark events in the history of the Jewish people. But running through this historical consciousness is reverence for the created order of the natural world, and for religious practice as the chief means of sustaining that order and experiencing its divine source and intensity. The Jewish holidays of Passover and Sukkot celebrate the renewal of life in spring and the abundance of the fall harvest. The dietary restrictions of kashrut are grounded in concern for the proper treatment of living things, and rules governing marital sexuality involve respect for natural functions of the human body. In both Jewish and Navajo thought, the forces and cycles of the natural world are understood to be full of religious meaning. In both cases, religious practice is the principal means of attending to this meaning, and of experiencing the divine power at work in the world.

SUGGESTIONS FOR FURTHER READING

Anita Diamant and Howard Cooper, *Living a Jewish Life: Jewish Traditions, Customs and Values for Today's Families* (New York: Harper Perennial, 1991).

Samuel H. Dresner, *The Jewish Dietary Laws* (New York: Burning Bush Press, 1959).

Irving Greenberg, *The Jewish Way: Living the Holidays* (New York: Touchstone, 1988).

Marc Lee Raphael, *Profiles in American Judaism: The Reform, Conservative, Orthodox, and Reconstructionist Traditions in Historical Perspective* (San Francisco: Harper & Row, 1984).

Michael Strassfeld, *The Jewish Holidays: A Guide and Commentary* (New York: Harper and Row, 1985).

Daniel B. Syme, *Why I Am a Reform Jew* (New York: Donald I. Fine, 1989).

Arthur Waskow, *Seasons of Our Joy* (New York: Bantam Press, 1982).

4

Islamic Salat

Nuri Ahmed, a university student in Alabama, rises each day at dawn in her parents' home to perform her morning *salat,* one of the five daily prayers that, for pious Muslims, make Islam a way of life. The procedures she follows in preparing for and performing salat are the same procedures followed by millions of Muslims around the world. Each morning, pious Muslims rise and cleanse themselves, rinsing hands, mouth, nose, and forearms, and then face, ears, and feet. Dressed in clean undergarments and loose-fitting clothes, they unroll individual-size prayer rugs and perform their prayers facing in the direction of Mecca, the Arabian city where Allah first gave his revelations to the prophet Muhammad. They bow first from the waist with hands above knees, then lift back and head until they are upright, and then drop down, with forehead, knees, and hands on the prayer rug. This posture of *sajda,* or prostration, demonstrates submission to Allah. Submission is the definition of the word Islam and the core element of Islamic practice.

After rising to a sitting posture, worshippers prostrate themselves again and then stand and repeat the procedure from
the beginning. After completing the whole cycle a second
time, they sit to recite the words of prayer, ending with the *shahadah*, the witness required of all Muslims, which includes the
words, *"la ilaha illa'llah* (There is no Allah but Allah)," and
"Muhammadun rasul Allah (Muhammad is his messenger)."

To Nuri, these words seem almost like breathing. Her parents often whispered the shahadah in her ear during her
infancy, and she began reciting the words back to her parents
before she understood their meaning. Many passages from the
Qur'an, the sacred book of Islam, are equally familiar, especially the opening *sura*, or chapter, praising Allah and asking
for his blessing. Each time they pray, or engage in any transaction, Muslims recite this sura, which has been translated in
English to read,

> In the name of Allah, the Beneficent, the Merciful.
> Praise be to Allah, Lord of the Worlds:
> The Beneficent, the Merciful:
> Owner of the Day of Judgement.
> Thee (alone) we worship; Thee (alone) we ask for help.
> Show us the straight path:
> The path of those whom Thou hast favored;
> Not (the path) of those who earn
> Thine anger nor of those who go astray.

Like other Muslims, Nuri and her family and friends recite
this passage in Arabic, as they do all other passages from the
Qur'an. And like other Muslims, they view translations of the
Qur'an in English or any other language as interpretations, not
to be confused with the Qur'an itself, which they believe is
divinely revealed both in form and content. According to Muslim belief, Allah spoke to the prophet Muhammad through the
angel Gabriel in Arabic, and Muhammad's transcriptions of
these revelations comprise the Qur'an. Thus Muslims revere the
Qur'an in its original Arabic as the definitive language of their
faith, a divine composition that is perfect, eternal, immutable,

exquisitely beautiful, and meant to be heard and recited exactly. In this respect, the Qur'an is different from the Christian Bible, which does not cease being the Bible when translated from its original languages. However much Christian believers look to the Bible for authority and guidance, they do not think of it as composed and spoken by God, as Muslims do the Qur'an.

Nuri believes this distinction is crucial for any comparison of Islam with Christianity. During class discussions in her religious studies course at the university, she has found that many Christians openly acknowledge the human authorship of the Bible. In her view, this admission is evidence of the Qur'an's superiority. She is aware that some of her fellow students believe that the Qur'an is just as much a human creation as the Bible, but she regards this attitude as an expression of the cynicism and religious ignorance prevalent in American society.

As Nuri recites the opening sura of the Qur'an in her morning prayers, she thinks about the presence of Allah's watchful eye over her life, and about the importance of being aware of Allah in everything that she does. "He is with you wherever you are," she recalls from another sura. She believes that Allah judges her *iman*, or faith, and that iman not only requires adherence to belief in Allah, his prophets, angels, revelations, and Day of Judgment, but also active fulfillment of the practices prescribed by the Qur'an and the *Sunnah*, the path of life exemplified by the prophet Muhammad. Nuri does not pray to Muhammad or regard him as a divine being, as Christians pray to Jesus and regard Jesus as the Son of God, but she does revere Muhammad as the prophet who received the Qur'an and defined the straight path of Islam. And like other Muslims, she cherishes the *Hadith*, the written accounts of the Prophet's life and teachings. Also like other Muslims, she cherishes the Five Pillars of faith, the five practices that have come to define the basis of Islamic religious life. These practices are shahadah, salat, almsgiving, fasting during the month of Ramadan, and pilgrimage to the holy site of Mecca, where Muhammad first heard the Qur'an and later returned in triumph before his death.

Like other Muslims, Nuri believes that Allah has had many prophets, including Adam, Noah, Abraham, Moses, and Jesus, and that some of them, like Moses and Jesus, have been entrusted with words of divine revelation as messengers of Allah. According to Islamic tradition, Allah sent his complete and final revelation to his prophet and messenger Muhammad, who was born in the western region of the Arabian Peninsula around the year 570 in the "common era" calendar of western culture. Muslims begin their calendar with the year corresponding to 622 C.E., when Muhammad moved from Mecca to Medina and established a religious culture based on the teachings of the Qur'an. Thus the year 2000 in the common era calendar of western culture is 1378 in the Islamic calendar.

After Muhammad's death in 632, Islam spread rapidly throughout the Middle East, extending across the Arabian Peninsula to Palestine, Syria, Mesopotamia, North Africa, Afghanistan, and into Iran by 656. During the "Dark Ages" of medieval Christendom, Muslim scholars preserved the writings of classical Greek and Roman authors, and fostered new developments in science, mathematics, and philosophy. Through trade, military force, and conversion, Islam spread to Spain, India, and beyond to what is now Malaysia, the Philippines, and Indonesia. Islamic empires dominated Turkey, Iran, and India in the sixteenth and seventeenth centuries. But Islamic rule was challenged in the eighteenth and nineteenth centuries as populations expanded, as social stress increased, and as British and European nations established colonies and spheres of influence in the nonwestern world and introduced new forms of economic development and exploitation. As a result of colonial and imperialistic domination by British and European powers in the nineteenth century, and of economic, military, and scientific domination by the United States and other western nations in the twentieth century, many Muslims today are suspicious of western power and both anxious and disdainful of western materialism. At the same time, Europe and the Americas have become part of the Islamic world as Muslim immigrants from Asia, Africa, and the Middle East have moved in large numbers to these places, and as a growing population of westerners convert to Islam.

One reason for Islam's increasing success in the United States is the relationship between some of its main concepts and well-known concepts in Christianity and Judaism. Muslims trace their faith back to Abraham, and to the covenant between God and Abraham, which was renewed by Moses on Mount Sinai, and later by the prophets of ancient Israel, including Jesus of Nazareth. Thus Muslims believe that Islam did not originate with the prophet Muhammad, but existed in the pure hearts of the founders of Judaism and Christianity. However, these religions became corrupted, Muslims believe, and many wrong ideas, false scriptures, and inappropriate practices became mixed in with the truth, and contributed to the waywardness and materialism of western culture. From this perspective, Islam is not so much a newcomer to the west as a recovery of the original faith embedded in Judaism and Christianity, which those religions have neglected and betrayed.

Like many of her Christian acquaintances, Nuri believes that God is all-knowing and that he sees directly into her heart. She has often felt God's presence during times of prayer. She believes that as well as watching her behavior, Allah knows the thoughts behind her actions, and whether or not they are wholehearted, sincere, and pure. Pure thoughts are those that are completely yoked to Allah, and involve no distracting element to take the place of Allah in the believer's heart. Such pure-heartedness is required not only during salat and other occasions of formalized religious ritual, but in other aspects of life as well. As Nuri understands it, this means that thoughts about popularity, wealth, sex, marriage, and her future should never distract from or corrupt her devotion to Allah. Thoughts about these things are completely acceptable, so long as they are framed in terms of submission to Allah. While popularity, wealth, sex, and marriage may all come to be part of her future, it is important that she not seek them as ends in themselves, but instead find them, if they are there for her, along the straight path of her submission to Allah.

This emphasis on submission does not mean that Nuri finds her life onerous or dominated by fear. To be sure, fulfilling her obligation to Allah is a serious and neverending business, and the eternal misery of Hell awaits those who fail, but as the opening sura of the Qur'an says, Allah is beneficent and merciful. Not only does he forgive the shortcomings of those who submit to him sincerely, but the process of submission can itself be a source of pleasure, and something like participation in a living work of art.

The pleasure and enjoyment of religious life is linked to the experience of *ihsan*, or beauty. Allah is ihsan, the Qur'an is ihsan, and the created world is ihsan. Humanity is a central part of this creation, and a pious Muslim respects the beauty of the human body and strives always to be attentive to its divine source. The pious Muslim also strives to bear witness to the beauty of Allah by doing what is beautiful, according to Allah's revelation in the Qur'an.

Salat is important to Nuri not only because it is a requirement of her faith, but also because it helps her focus on the beauty of Allah, and on her own participation in that beauty. The full-body prostration of sajda expresses the beauty of the human form, consciously centered on submission to Allah, just as the words of prayer express the beauty of human desire when consciously centered on submission to Allah. Sajda is the model for how she should act during the rest of the day. Thus Nuri believes that everything she does with her body, and everything her heart desires, should ultimately center on submission to Allah and bear witness to his beauty.

For this reason, Nuri is very attentive to how she dresses. She is well aware that the clothes she wears are a form of communication to others, and she wants to communicate her commitment to Allah. Nuri is also very conscious of her own beauty; indeed, because of the emphasis on women's natural beauty in Islam, she is more confident of her beauty than many American women her age. She is also more concerned than many American women not to divert men's attention improperly, and she is eager to avoid exposing her beauty in ways that are not pleasing to Allah. To this end, she dresses very modestly in loose-fitting trousers and long-sleeved, high-necked shirts that conceal her flesh and obscure the outline of her body. Outside her home, she wears a *hajib*, or head covering, that hides her neck, and ears, and hair.

Nuri's mother, Sumreen, has never worn the hajib. In Egypt, where she and her husband Asad were married and started their family, Sumreen embraced many aspects of western culture in anticipation of moving to the United States, and dressed modestly in western-style clothes, as she does now. Unlike her daughter, Sumreen grew up in a Muslim culture and never felt that her religious identity was something she needed constantly to demonstrate. When she and Asad moved to the United States, being Muslim was as much a fact of life as being Egyptian, and she has never experienced the same existential need to prove her faith as her daughter. But she does understand what her daughter is going through. In fact, she is concerned about her children's faith in ways she has never been about her own. She is especially concerned about her eldest son, a high school student whom she and her husband cannot protect as carefully as they do their daughters. All three of her children are growing up in a society that is at once more secular and more Christian than Egyptian society, and Sumreen fears that if they assimilate to this society, and identify with American culture and with the outlook of their schoolmates, they will lose their faith in Allah and their respect for the Qur'an. So she supports Nuri's intense religious vigilance, and her wearing of the hajib.

Nuri is one of a growing number of young women in different parts of the world who are choosing to cover their bodies to demonstrate their Islamic faith. Beyond a common concern to restrict exposure of female beauty in religiously sanctioned ways, the motivations behind this increasingly widespread phenomenon vary somewhat from one culture to another. In Cairo, for example, young women attending university classes and pursuing employment cover themselves not only to express their commitment to Allah, but also to make a place for themselves alongside men who may be uncomfortable with the idea of women pursuing the same kind of work that they do. These men would feel freer to treat their female colleagues with disrespect if their dress could be considered provocative. Thus men's tendency to disrespect is held in check by women's choice of a form of dress that clearly announces commitment to Allah.

In the United States, motivations for covering also involve concern for modesty and desire to command men's respect, but here, the custom of women working alongside men is taken more for granted, and uncovered women are not subject to open harassment as often as they are in Muslim countries. However, American women live in a society where displays of female sexuality are commonplace and highly commercialized, and where social pressures on young women to be sexually active and sexually demonstrative are considerable. In this context, covering sends the message that one does not condone or participate in the climate of sexual freedom and openness that seems to characterize American culture.

Nuri and her friends believe that the strict moral behavior they follow ultimately makes them freer than many of their female peers, whom they regard as sexually driven and often desperate. They criticize American culture for constantly pressuring women to lower themselves to the status of sexual objects, and they believe that Islam does more to liberate women than western society. They point out that women played important roles in the life of Muhammad and in the early establishment of Islam, and that the Qur'an insists on respectful treatment of women, and on women's rights to inheritance and property ownership. As far as Nuri and her Muslim friends are concerned, Islam is essentially a feminist religion, although its potential to liberate women is not fully realized in the world today.

The belief in Islam's power to liberate women, which is so important to Nuri and her friends, is similar to ideas held by Orthodox Jewish women. Some strictly Orthodox women wear wigs outside the home to cover the natural beauty of their hair, and consider exposure of hair, elbows, knees, or chest to be a kind of nakedness that is inappropriate for them as religious women. Moreover, women who have converted to Orthodox Judaism in the United States often feel, as Nuri and her Muslim friends do, that their religion offers a good alternative to the climate of sexual promiscuity and exploitation they believe to be prevalent in American society. From the perspectives of both groups of women, covering one's body is associated with freedom and respect.

Nuri and her friends acknowledge that women have also been treated as sexual objects in Muslim cultures, and have little patience with some of the restrictions imposed on women in the name of Islam. For example, they ridicule the prohibition against women driving cars in Saudi Arabia, pointing out that, in Muhammad's day, women drove camels, which were more difficult to handle. They argue that such unjust restrictions against women's activities are the result of *cultural* tendencies prevalent in the Middle East and North Africa, and not necessarily linked to the *religion* of Islam.

This distinction between religion and culture has been crucial to Nuri's understanding of women's role in Islam. However, it seemed at first to run counter to some of the ideas put forward in her religious studies class, where religion is defined as a form of culture. When she first encountered it, this cultural approach to religion left Nuri feeling that her belief in the truth of Islam was being challenged by a western ideology of religious and cultural relativism. But when she discussed the matter with one of her religious teachers, he drew her attention to the fact that the Arabic word *din* can refer to any religion, including the true religion described in the Qur'an. They agreed that, if religion is viewed as a form of culture, it might also be argued that some cultures are based in submission to Allah as prescribed in the Qur'an, while others are not. And among those cultures that have declared themselves Islamic, the degree of adherence to Qur'anic rule varies dramatically.

Belief in the existence of Allah-given rules and structures for human life links Islam more closely to Judaism than to many forms of Christianity. Muslims and Jews share a concern for religious law that distances them from Christians who believe that grace is the defining factor of faith, and that the power of grace supersedes obligation to religious law. While Jews locate religious law in the Torah, the Talmud, and in rabbinic interpretations of these compiled through the centuries, Muslims locate Islamic law, or *Shariah*, in the Qur'an, the Sunna, and in legal arguments based on them that have been compiled through the centuries by Islamic scholars. The contents of these two bodies of religious law vary importantly in detail, but in both traditions, rules for governing behavior play a central role in defining religious faith. In Islam, Shariah literally means the "road leading to water," an apt metaphor from a desert culture expressing the importance of following religious commands and prohibitions.

In both Islamic and Jewish traditions, religious law facilitates respect for the created order of the world, including the natural cycles, functions, and pleasures of the human body, all of which are understood to glorify Allah. Like pious Muslims, pious Jews cherish the practice of religion as a means of structuring daily life and nurturing experience of Allah. Thus in both cases, the performance of ritual not only fulfills Allah's commands and regulates behavior, but also creates a form of spiritual awareness that enables the believer to live the whole of life with more consciousness of Allah than would otherwise be possible.

The difference between Muslim and Christian ideas about the relationship between faith and law involves a conflict in belief about Jesus of Nazareth. While Christians believe he is the Son of God who brings the grace that triumphs over law, in the eyes of many Muslims, such ideas are idolatrous perversions of the monotheistic principle that "there is no Allah but Allah." Christian belief in a triune, or three-dimensioned, godhead—Father, Son, and Holy Ghost—seems to many Muslims to be a form of polytheism, and hence a corruption of the pure monotheism taught by Allah's prophets, including Jesus himself.

While Christians agree that God transcends human comprehension and that his nature is incomparable, Muslims insist on these points more strictly. This insistence is reflected in the Muslim's avoidance of prayers directed to Muhammad. While Christians offer prayers to Jesus Christ in the belief that he can intercede for them, Muslims insist on Muhammad's humanity and do not appeal to him for intercession.

The strictness of the interpretation of monotheism in Islam is exemplified in the contrast between the religious art of Islam and that of Roman Catholicism. While Catholic churches contain at least one image of Christ that is designed and displayed as a focus for prayer and worship, mosques do not contain any images. The Islamic tendency to avoid visual representation of human and animal forms reflects the belief that the nature of Allah is beyond human comprehension. Although depictions of Muhammad do exist in Islamic art, they are never displayed in a *mosque*, a Muslim place of prayer and study, or in ways that would confuse a worshiper into thinking that Allah was like him, or like any human being.

Geometric abstractions are the preferred form of sacred art in Islam, and can be seen on mosques around the world. These designs express the perfection and beauty of Allah as well as his transcendence of human forms. Mosques are often places of great artistry, architecturally pleasing and, in many cases, embellished with calligraphy from the Qur'an and elaborate "Arabesque" tile and grillwork. For the Muslim no less than the Christian or Jew, Allah is beautiful, the world created by him is beautiful, and religious ritual nurtures the believer's awareness and experience of this beauty.

In certain important respects, the Muslim concept of ihsan is similar to the Navajo emphasis on beauty, or hozho. As you will recall, Navajo religion centers on awareness of hozho as the chief characteristic of the created world, and on concern to embody this quality in one's thought and action. The ceremonies of Navajo religion are devoted to restoring hozho in places and persons where its harmonious balance has been disturbed. Thus Navajo sandpaintings recreate hozho by invoking the presence of Holy People and directing their powers in certain ways.

Although Navajo Holy People are, in some respects, comparable to the angels described in the Qur'an and Hadith, Muslims would reject Navajo stories that attribute the creation of the world to the Holy People. Muslims would also reject the Navajo belief that recovery of the harmony of creation depends on human beings, who have the ability, and responsibility, to manipulate divine power. But they share with the Navajo a sense that beauty is a fundamental aspect of the created world. They also share with the Navajo a profound sense of responsibility to embody beauty in action and thought. Thus in her understanding of ihsan as doing as well as apprehending what is beautiful, Nuri's performance of salat centers on a powerful sense of commitment to the beauty of Allah and his creations that is akin to the Navajo investment in the harmony of the created world.

SUGGESTIONS FOR FURTHER READING

Leila Ahmed, *Women and Gender in Islam: Historical Roots of a Modern Debate* (New Haven: Yale University Press, 1992).

Frederich Mathewson Denny, *An Introduction to Islam* (New York: Macmillan, 1985).

John L. Esposito, *Islam: The Straight Path* 2nd ed. (New York: Oxford University Press, 1991).

Yvonne Yazbeck Haddad and Adair T. Lummis, *Islamic Values in the United States: A Comparative Study* (New York: Oxford University Press, 1987).

Michael A. Koszegi and J. Gordon Melton, *Islam in North America: A Sourcebook* (New York: Garland Publishing, Inc., 1992).

Sanchiko Murata and William C. Chittick, *The Vision of Islam* (New York: Paragon House, 1994).

Parents Manual, A Guide for Muslim Parents Living in North America (Indianapolis: American Trust Publications, 1976).

5

Puja to the Hindu
Goddess Devi

Jaya Masand and her friend Jennifer enter the small upstairs room in Jaya's home that is set aside for *puja*, or worship. On a low altar at the front of the room stands a six-inch *murti*, or image and embodiment, of the mother goddess Devi. Jaya joins the palms of her hands and bows to Devi's murti, which is made out of painted wood. On one side of the goddess is a murti of Devi's consort Siva, and on the other side a photograph of Jaya's *guru*, or religious teacher, with a garland of flowers draped over the frame. Hung from the wall behind are two posters of Devi, one of her smiling benignly, and another with eight arms, each holding a weapon or some other power object, brandished in the process of killing the great Buffalo Demon who threatened to destroy the universe. Other gods tried to destroy the Demon, but even Siva failed. Jaya turns to her friend Jennifer and explains, "Devi is the savior of the universe. She is our Mother. She protects us, and brings us happiness, wealth, and good luck. She is powerful and beautiful. And she intervenes in our lives when we need her support or guidance, often at moments when we do not expect her."

When she comes home from work each afternoon, Jaya prepares dinner for her parents, who live with her, and for her teenage son and daughter if they are home. Before making dinner for herself, she heads upstairs to bathe and change, and to spend half an hour or so with Devi. One or more members of her family sometimes join her puja, but tonight she is accompanied only by Jennifer, who works with Jaya as a librarian in Houston.

"Devi is an honored guest in our home," Jaya explains. "We keep fresh fruit and flowers to please her," Jaya continues, pointing to the purple blossoms and grapes in a brass bowl on the altar. "We bow to her and thank her for coming, sing her favorite songs, wash her feet and hands and face, and light incense for her." Jaya opens a wooden box with elaborate carving on the lid, selects a stick of incense, fixes it upright in a small brass pot with four legs, and lights it with a match. As the sweet smell of sandalwood begins to drift through the room, she places the pot on the altar and bows again to Devi. "After I finish singing and attending to Devi, I sometimes talk with her about my problems; at other times I just sit quietly with her. She helps me in many ways, directing my thoughts toward certain things, and shielding me and my family from harm.

"Once she appeared to me when I did not expect it," Jaya confides. "It was in India, just before my children and I were leaving for the States. Many people looked down on me because my husband had left me, so I was coming to the States to live with my sister and her husband, and to start a new life. I was at the railway station in Delhi when suddenly I noticed a little girl walking along beside me. This little girl turned her face up and gave me the most beautiful and comforting smile, as if she were saying, You have a fine future ahead, and I am very pleased. Then she turned away into the crowd and disappeared. No one knew who she was, where she had come from, or where she had gone. After she left, I thought it must have been Devi. She can take any form — a little girl, an old man, whatever she likes. But you know it is Devi because her beauty and power shine out, and touch your heart. When she came to me at the railway station, I knew that my journey was blessed, that Devi was helping us, and that things would work out well for us in America. And so they have," Jaya concludes, "My children are healthy, I have a good job, my sister and her family live nearby, and my parents came from India to live with me, and helped me buy this house."

"I see how much Devi means to you," says Jennifer, "and I sense that this room is a holy place, as well as a very pleasant spot to gather your thoughts at the end of the day. But I don't understand exactly what you believe about the statue of Devi. Do you honor it as a guest because it *is* Devi? Or does it just depict Devi," Jennifer goes on, "and so you honor it as a way of expressing your desire to honor her?" Jaya laughs. "No, No, this murti is not just a reminder of Devi. It has been made real through a special ritual. But your question shows that have the mind of a scholar, full of concern for analysis and precise distinctions. You would like Hindu philosophy because it is rich in discussion of such distinctions. However, many Hindu saints have said that detailed knowledge about such things is not necessary; all you really need to do is love God. But yes, to answer your question, this really *is* Devi," Jaya says. "My guru performed a ceremony that brought *jiva*, or life, into the image. We used my *prana*, or breath, to bring jiva. As a result, the life of this particular murti is linked closely to my own. But of course the prana that comes from me does not really belong to me. Prana is everywhere, and everywhere the same. Like *Brahman*, the universal self, which it expresses, prana is universal and impersonal."

The two women sit quietly for a moment, both looking at Devi. Jennifer clears her throat and asks, "What then is the relationship between Brahman, the universal self manifest in prana, and Devi, the great goddess who saves the world, protects you, and is manifest in this image?"

"Brahman is ultimate reality; Brahman is the absolute. Devi is a form the absolute takes. To me she is the supreme form, the ultimate personification of the nature and power of life. It is much easier to worship her than to worship the impersonal Brahman. But they are both real. You might say they occupy different levels of reality. The existence of one does not take away from the existence of the other any more than the fact that we all breathe takes away from our individuality. As I see the world, Devi is the chief of all the personified deities. But other Hindus worship Siva or Krsna or Rama as the chief deity. Each of us sees the world somewhat differently, but that does not mean that your way is true and my way is false. At the impersonal level, all of these different ways of seeing and worshiping finally meet and dissolve in the absolute."

Bhaktimarga, or the path of loving devotion to a personified god, is the path most Hindus follow in quest of blessings, happiness, and salvation. Puja is the main ritual ingredient in the form of Hinduism identified with loving devotion to God. As worship of a personified god, puja involves prayers for happiness and blessing in this world and also for union with divine reality beyond this world. In its embrace of both types of prayer, bhakti Hinduism surmounts an old division in India between priestly traditions that are fundamentally this-worldly in orientation, focusing on health, safety, and security, and philosophical traditions that are fundamentally other worldly in orientation, focusing on withdrawal from the world and understanding of the illusory nature of material reality. Often inconsistently mixed, but equally stressed, these two aspects of bhakti Hinduism comprise one of its most important and distinguishing features.

In conversation over tea and sweet cakes later that evening, Jennifer asks Jaya's parents how devotion to Devi is different from devotion to other Hindu deities. Jaya's father, Kapil, answers that the various forms of Hindu devotion are like the various denominations within Christianity. Each group differs from others in important ways, but there is much underlying ground of agreement.

As Jennifer learns from reading about Hinduism at the library, scholars often divide the Hindu sects into three

branches, *Vishnavites, Shivites,* or *Shaktas.* Vishnavites worship
one of the many incarnations of the god Visnu, Shivites worship the god Siva, and Shaktas worship the mother goddess
Devi, also known as Kali or Shakti. The majority of Hindu worshippers are devotees of Visnu in his incarnation as Krsna or
Rama. Krsna is playful, erotic, and lyrical, sometimes portrayed as the Divine Child, and sometimes as the flute player
and lover of the maiden cowherders, called *gopis.* Krsna is
often portrayed with his favorite consort, the beautiful gopi
Radha. He is the principal deity in the *Bhagavadgita,* which
many Hindus take as a guide for living. For many of his devotees, Krsna is a savior, and many Hindus believe Christ to be
one of his incarnations of their Lord.

Rama is also a form of Visnu. This majestic warrior is the
hero of the popular *Ramayana* and the beloved husband of
the faithful Sita, whose devotion to Rama is also storied in the
Ramayana. In recent years, Rama and Sita have been portrayed in popular Indian films. Rama has also functioned as
the patron deity of right-wing Hindu nationalists who object to
secular government in India and believe that Muslims, Christians, and others should not have the same rights as Hindus.
In one incident, followers of Rama destroyed an Islamic
mosque built on the site of the legendary birthplace of Rama.

As the central deity in the second branch of Hindu sectarian-
ism, Siva is one of the most ancient Hindu deities, and most
commonly worshiped in south India, where some of the oldest
forms of Hinduism still persist. Like other deities, Siva is a savior. Because he was willing to drink the poison that threatened
to destroy life, pictures often show his neck blue from the poison's stain. Siva wields powers of both creation and destruction.
While his name translates as "benevolent and gracious one," he
is often portrayed as wrathful, terrible, and destructive. As the
Nataraja, or Lord of the Dance, he liberates the world through a
cosmic dance that is both creative and destructive. As an ascetic
who masters both creative and destructive impulses, he offers
immortality to his followers. In temples and shrines where he
is worshiped, Siva is always represented by a stone *lingam,* a

phallic-shaped murti representing the god's subtle nature and latent sexual potency. Thus in Jaya Masand's shrine, Siva is represented by a lingam, while the goddess Devi is represented by a statue shaped in the figure of a woman.

Like Siva, Devi is associated with both creative and destructive power. In earlier centuries, notorious bands of "left-handed" Kali worshippers identified themselves exclusively with the destructive aspect of the mother goddess, and performed bloody human sacrifices in her name. However, the vast majority of Devi (and Kali) worshippers emphasize the creative, kind, and beautiful aspects of her nature while always being aware of her destructive side. The influential nineteenth-century saint Ramakrishna was a devotee of Devi, and famous for falling into ecstatic trances, overcome by Devi's beauty.

As a proponent of *Advaita Vedanta,* a philosophical outlook based on the idea that the material world is the outer manifestation of a single spiritual principle or force, Ramakrishna preached that all Hindu sects were essentially the same, and that differences in belief were finally trivial compared to the quest for spiritual realization, which he believed was the common ground of all religion. During the 1893 World's Fair in Chicago, Ramakrishna's disciple Vivekananda was the first official emissary of Hinduism in the United States, and since that time, Americans attracted to Hinduism have tended to embrace the Advaita Vedanta outlook, including practitioners of Transcendental Meditation, brought to the United States by Mahesh Yagi Maharishi, as well as members of the International Society of Krsna Consciousness, or ISKON, most commonly known as Hari Krishnas, after their chant, "Hari, Hari Krishna."

The term *Vedanta* literally means the end of the *Vedas.* The oldest scriptures of India, the Vedas are comprised of hymns to the ancient gods of the earth and heavens, and procedures for sacrifices and other priestly rituals aimed at securing their cooperation. Vedanta emphasizes spiritual knowledge rather than priestly sacrifice as a means to salvation. The path of spiritual knowledge involves philosophical study and the practice of one or more of a variety of forms of *yoga*, systems of meditation, diet, and physical activity. When pursued as a means to salvation, yoga leads to experiential knowledge of the absolute. Much of Hindu philosophy is based on the assumption that *atman*, the spiritual essence at the core of the individual self, is the same as Brahman, the absolute, universal, and impersonal self within all living beings. However, disagreement exists about the ultimate nature of the material world and its relationship to Brahman. Followers of Advaita Vedanta believe that all of reality is ultimately spiritual in nature, and that the material world is, finally, an illusion.

While Jaya Masand is both a devotee of the goddess Devi and an Advaita Vedantist, other Hindus view their gods as existing above and apart from material reality. Thus many Hindus who give pujas to a personal god do not share the monistic outlook of Advaita Vedanta. As a result, they are less willing than Jaya to equate one deity or form of worship with another.

Hinduism is well known for its ability to accommodate a wide variety of different, and even conflicting, beliefs and practices. In fact, such a multitude of beliefs and practices exists within this religious arena that it would be more accurate to refer to Hinduisms as a plural noun referring to an enormous collection of religions rather than to Hinduism as a single faith. To some extent, this observation can be made of other great religions as well—there are many Christianities and many Judaisms as well as many Hinduisms. But unlike Christians and Jews, Hindus have not, until recently, held any concept of a core faith to which different branches adhered. Thus until westerners introduced the term Hinduism in the nineteenth century to define the religion indigenous to India, Hindu had referred to people in the subcontinent of India and not to religion at all. Beginning with Mahatma Gandhi in the mid-twentieth century, Indian nationalists embraced the term Hinduism to distinguish the spiritual outlook of Indians from western colonialism, and to engender national identity and pride.

But while the concept of Hinduism is quite new, the religious beliefs and practices associated with that concept are among the oldest in the world. The *Rgveda*, the earliest collection of Vedic hymns, was composed around 1200 B.C.E. As a system of priestly ritual, the Vedas reflect the authority of Aryan invaders and immigrants into India, and both their assimilation into and dominance over earlier populations. Beginning in the ninth century before the common era, wandering ascetics turned away from the Vedic system of priestly sacrifices in search of experiential knowledge of ultimate reality, and developed a variety of philosophical systems, including Buddhism and *Jainism*, a religion of strict nonviolence founded by the sage Mahavira in the sixth century before the common era. Around the eighth century of the common era, Shankara and other philosophers worked to define orthodox beliefs and practices over against Buddhism and Jainism, and established various systems of Vedanta thought along with respect for the Vedas and the priests who performed Vedic rites. At the same time, popular devotions to deities not prominent or, in some cases, even mentioned in the Vedas flourished alongside both Vedantic and Vedic disciplines.

In addition to their emotional appeal, these popular devotions have been attractive because of their openness to and respect for all members of society. In contrast, both Vedantic and Vedic practices have been reserved for members of the upper castes, and especially for the hereditary caste of priests known as *Brahmins*. In former times, only Brahmins were literate and permitted to read the ancient scriptures containing ritual formulae. Even today, those who invest in Brahmanic ritual participate in a worldview that presumes Brahmins to be closer to salvation than other people, and the only ones eligible to perform many rituals. But this system of priestly orthopraxy has often been challenged by spiritual reformers critical of the emphasis on arcane procedure as well as the exclusion of the vast majority of people from full participation in religious life. Spiritual reformers like Ramakrishna have focused instead on the importance of bhakti, maintaining that love of God is sufficient for full religious life. As a means of expressing this love of God, puja is a ritual alternative to orthoprax Brahmanism. Unlike Brahmanic ritual, puja can be performed by any religious person, regardless of birth or wealth.

This distinction between the formalism of Brahmanic ritual and the devotionalism of bhakti puja can lead to useful comparisons with other religions whose practices we have discussed. The Navajo, for example, whose sandpaintings we discussed in the first chapter, are like orthoprax Brahmins in their insistence on correct performance of ritual. Like orthoprax Brahmin priests, Navajo singers seek to improve the fortunes of their patrons by means of ritual action, and are relatively indifferent to what bhaktas would call piety — cultivating an existential state of pure devotional love is no more a part of Navajo ceremony than Brahmanic ritual. However, Navajo practitioners do believe that action flows out of speech and thought, and that thought works through speech and ritual action, and ultimately determines their effect. Similarly, orthoprax Brahmins believe that certain words and chants carry spiritual force, especially when manifest through ritual action.

Interesting comparisons can also be drawn with regard to Hindu and Navajo conceptions of the unity of god. In Navajo tradition, Changing Woman is a personification of the earth whose life is identified with the changing seasons. Although she is not worshiped in the same way that Devi is by her devotees, Changing Woman is like Devi in representing the spiritual force within life and death. Both Hindus and Navajos can conceptualize the spiritual nature of life as a single divine person, and at the same time recognize a plurality of spirits in their beliefs, stories, and ritual activities. Thus during ceremonies, Navajo singers negotiate with various spirits, each of whom is believed to influence a particular part of the natural and social environment. Similarly, puja to the goddess Devi does not exclude puja to other deities, or respect for their power over different aspects of life.

Catholicism also contains important similarities to Hinduism, including a strong element of devotional piety not emphasized in Navajo ceremony. Like Jaya Masand, Catholic worshippers believe that God is one, eternal, and absolute, but also manifest in personified form in a deity who imparts both this-worldly blessings and eternal salvation. Hindu puja is similar to the Catholic Eucharist in its focus on the worshipper's devotion to a personified god, and in its effectiveness in bringing worshippers to an experience of the presence of their god. Hindu puja is also similar to Catholic devotion to saints. Although official Catholic teaching would emphasize that saints are only mediators between believers and God and not deities themselves, in actual practice Catholics pray to particular saints in much the same way that Hindus pray to particular gods, asking for blessings of various kinds and venerating images of their holy presence.

Practitioners of both Hindu bhakti and Roman Catholic devotion resist ritual action that is merely formulaic, and without emotional commitment. But in addition to a commitment to religious devotion that they share with Hindu bhaktas, Catholics also rely on the correct and carefully legitimated performance of ritual by priests who, like orthoprax Brahmins, are thoroughly trained in established procedure. In contrast to the exactness and professionalism of priestly performance in both Hinduism and Catholicism, puja is more flexible, innovative, and personalized. The Devi puja that Jaya performs is tailored to her needs and experiences, and proceeds without priestly supervision, much like Catholic devotion to saints.

In Judaism, the most intense forms of devotion to God coexist with concern for the meticulous practice of religion. Thus while Jews are like bhaktas in their belief that religious observance should express and nurture devotion to God, and Jewish pietistic traditions have nurtured experiences of the presence of God similar to Ramakrishna's religious ecstasies, orthopraxy is equally respected. Especially in Orthodox Jewish circles, Jews are like Brahmins in their conformity to rules prescribed in ancient scripture and in their exact observance of religious procedure.

With respect to their investment in orthopraxy, Jews can also be like Brahmins in their assumption of special religious status compared to other groups. Thus Jewish ideas about being a "chosen people" bear certain similarities to Brahmanic concepts of caste. As a result of their self-conception as descendants of the prophets, priests, and kings of Israel, and as a result of the responsibility they undertake to observe the religious laws revealed to their ancestors and outlined in the Torah, Jews often feel privileged to enjoy a special relationship with the divine. Brahmins have also felt privileged as a result of their birth, and as a result of the responsibility they undertake to perform the rituals outlined in ancient scripture. But if both Jews and Brahmins have understood themselves to be set apart from other groups because of their concepts of religious obligation and privilege, these concepts have functioned differently in history and society. While the religious obligations and privileges of Brahmins have often brought high social status and respect from other members of their society, belief in Jewish chosenness has not secured Jews a stable position of recognized religious privilege in a larger society, but has often offended more powerful groups, and led to the persecution of Jews.

Reformers within both traditions have criticized the elitism associated with their traditions of special religious status and privilege. Some Hindus born and educated as Brahmins have become influential bhakti leaders opposed to both the exclusivism and the formalism of Hindu orthopraxy. In a similar vein, reformist Jews have been committed to breaking out of the insularity of Jewish orthodoxy, emphasizing the obligation to *tikkun olum*, repairing the world, as a responsibility that requires commitment to social justice and human equality throughout the world.

The biggest differences between Jews and Hindus involve beliefs about the nature of God. Jewish monotheism is less complicated than Christian monotheism, which recognizes one God in three parts (Father, Son, and Holy Spirit), while Hindu monotheism is compatible with worship of several different deities. Like Jaya's Devi, the God of the Jews is a personal god, with characteristics befitting personhood—Devi is a kind and beautiful mother, and the God of the Jews is a just and loving ruler. But the Jewish God is never embodied in material form as Devi and other deities are depicted, or as Christ is in Catholic homes and churches. While Catholics believe in the same God as Jews and share many of the same stories about him, Catholic worship is closer to bhakti Hinduism than is Judaism.

Many of the same differences that obtain between Hinduism and Judaism also obtain between Hinduism and Islam. Emphasis on the unified nature of God is no less strong in Islam than in Judaism, and Islamic prohibitions against representations of God are no less strict. Indeed, in some respects the contrast between Hinduism and Islam is greater than that between Hinduism and Judaism. Islamic resistance to any form of theological liberalism is much more complete than Jewish resistance; thus belief in the revealed nature of the Qur'an is widely accepted among Muslims, while many Jews believe that their scriptures were written by men. Moreover, while the Qur'an states that God is as close to man as his jugular, and Islamic mystics have sometimes experienced the presence of God so intensely that they felt at one with him, Muslims insist even more than Jews on the ineradicable gap between God and human beings, whom the Qur'an describes as just clots of blood. This emphasis on the gap between God and humanity stands in sharp contrast to the widespread Hindu belief that God can be found within the self.

Along with these fundamental differences, pious devotion is a common ingredient in both Hindu and Muslim religions. While the embodiment of God in Jaya's Devi puja would be anathema to Muslims, the simplicity and heartfelt intensity of her devotion is similar to that of Muslima Nuri Ahmed, and each derives from her prayers a comparable sense of direction and well-being. Like bhakti Hindus, Muslims emphasize both the necessity and sufficiency of heartfelt devotion to God.

Indeed, the bhakti tradition in Hinduism exerted significant influence on Islam in India, and pious mystics played a central role in disseminating Islam in eastern Asia. The egalitarian aspect of bhakti Hinduism also finds correspondence in Islam. Like bhaktas who believe that loving God is all one needs to break through the confusions and constraints of this life and attain salvation, Muslims believe that God judges each individual not according to birth, wealth, or status, but by faith alone.

SUGGESTIONS FOR LISTENING AND FURTHER READING

Natalia Isayeva, *Shankara and Indian Philosophy* (Albany: State University of New York Press, 1993).

Carl Jackson, *Vedanta for the West: The Ramakrishna Movement in the United States* (Bloomington: University of Indiana Press, 1994).

Klaus K. Klostermaier, *A Survey of Hinduism* (Albany: State University of New York Press, 1989).

Gregory Kozlowski, Walter Harrelson, Mike Hassell, and Pat Childs, *Hinduism*, narrated by Ben Kingsley. Religion, Scriptures & Spirituality, The Audio Classics Series (Nashville: Knowledge Products, 1994).

Bansi Pandit, *The Hindu Mind: Fundamentals of Hindu Religion and Philosophy for All Ages*, 2d ed. (Glen Ellyn, Ill: B & V Enterprises, 1993).

Joanne Punzo Waghorne and Norman Cutler, eds., *Gods of Flesh, Gods of Stone: The Embodiment of Divinity in India* (Chambersburg, Penn.: Anima Publications, 1985).

6

Buddhist Zazen

In a spare room with white walls, a polished wood floor, and three long windows covered in pleated white shades, Ned Lundstrom and two of his students are doing *zazen*, the sitting meditation characteristic of Zen Buddhism. The practice of meditation is central to Zen Buddhism—indeed, *Zen* literally means meditation—and zazen is the most common and important form. But Zen incorporates other forms of meditation as well, including tea ceremonialism, rock gardening, flower arranging, calligraphy, manual labor, and virtually any other form of activity that concentrates mind and body on the "conditioned" nature of existence. The ultimate goal of all these forms of meditation is *satori*, or enlightenment, which Zen Buddhists describe as a clear-sightedness unmarred by the self's longing for permanence and unconditionedness. While only a few practitioners actually attain satori, a larger number experience *kensho*, a taste of the enlightened state of mind that is genuine, but not yet sustainable.

Ned Lundstrom and his students sit on round hard pillows, or *zafus*, covered in black cloth. The students try to emulate their teacher's posture, straightening their spines, pushing their heads up, holding their arms slightly away from the body as if, as Ned had instructed, they were holding eggs between their arms and torsos. Their hands are arranged in the oval *mudra* position, left hand over right, with the middle joints of middle fingers touching and thumbs with a hair's breadth of space between, in front of the *hara*, or source of energy and breath in the abdomen. Only Ned can manage to thoroughly relax his shoulders and cross his legs in the full lotus position, with right foot resting on left thigh and left foot resting on right thigh, and this position is sometimes painful for him, even after ten years of practice. But he always sits zazen in full lotus because the structure of the position has a balanced and centering effect, and because he knows that in this position, many others have attained wisdom and insight.

Brian and Sarah are struggling with their zazen, feeling uncomfortable even in half-lotus position, with only one foot up on the opposite thigh and the other crossed under the opposite thigh. They are students in Ned's course on eastern philosophy at college, and interested in learning more about Buddhism. When he mentioned some of his own experiences sitting zazen during class one day, the two of them approached him afterwards about the possibility of sitting with him, and Ned agreed, inviting them to his house near campus for a session of sitting and then tea.

From what they have read and learned in class, the students know that the practice of meditation is central to Zen Buddhism and that, from the Zen perspective, enlightenment is something that one prepares for through practice. Although Zen Buddhists define satori and kensho as intuitive breakthroughs that surpass logic and do not automatically result from the effort to meditate, they are deeply committed to zazen, and believe that enlightenment is most often realized through its discipline.

As Brian tries to get comfortable in Mr. Lundstrom's *zendo*, or place for zazen, he recalls one of the required readings from class, a book of lectures by the Soto Zen Master Shunryu

Suzuki, who established the Zen Center of San Francisco and the first Zen monastery in the western world at Tassajara. This famous *roshi*, or Zen teacher, talked about the importance of posture in zazen, and described the interdependence of posture and religious insight as an example of the nondualism so important to Buddhist philosophy. Correcting his students' idea that assuming the approved posture was merely a means to attaining what he called "the right state of mind," Suzuki roshi asserted that, "To take this posture is itself to have the right state of mind." Unable to assume the right posture, or even to find a similar posture in which he feels comfortable, Brian becomes aware that he is having a very concrete experience of how far away he is from the right state of mind.

Sarah is having another kind of difficulty. She feels like her mind is going to explode, and the effort she is imposing to keep her body in an upright posture feels like rigid containment, and nothing like the peace and tranquility she has read about in discussions of Buddhist meditation and enlightenment. She is intensely anxious, and had never expected that sitting zazen would make her feel so emotionally out of control. Perhaps sensing her discomfort and trying to be helpful, Mr. Lundstrom draws a deep and audible breath. Breathe, Sarah thinks, I've got to breathe more deeply. I'm supposed to breathe from my hara and not just from the chest. Yes, she thinks, I can focus my mind by thinking about my breath. And a different saying from Suzuki roshi occurs to her: "What we call 'I' is just a swinging door which moves when we inhale and when we exhale." It is the breath coming in and going out that is most important, she thinks. And along with breath, thoughts and feelings are coming in and going out. There's really no "I" that's losing its grip here. Then why, she wonders sarcastically, am "I" having such a hard time with this?

After sitting for about forty minutes, Mr. Lundstrom draws his knees together and bows toward his students, touching his forehead to the floor. Unfolding their legs, the students reciprocate with bows to him. They all stand, stretch a bit, smile quietly at each other, and file downstairs to the kitchen for tea.

Sitting at the kitchen table, Sarah and Brian watch their teacher's movements as he sets out biscuits and cheese, and prepares their green tea. Both of them are struck by the effortless flow of these arrangements, and by their simple beauty. As he sips from a round white cup, Brian's mind is clear and his senses are sharp. He is aware of the tea's aroma filling his nostrils, and of its smooth texture and deep flavor. He recalls the story of the Zen master who responded to a request from a disciple for inspirational words with the single word "Attention!" When the disciple expressed his dissatisfaction with this response and his hope for a fuller exposition, the roshi shouted, "Attention! Attention! Attention!"

After enjoying tea together, Mr. Lundstrom pulls a wood-sided box about half an inch high to the center of the kitchen table and sets down a small wooden rake beside it. Inside the low box is a miniature rock garden, with five small stones of different shapes and colors placed in one corner, on a bed of sand raked in fine parallel lines that curve out from the rocks like waves. As Sarah studies the arrangement, she is struck by how this garden of dry still rocks resembles a seascape of flowing water. She is struck, too, by how such a tiny, humanly controlled scene could evoke an image of such huge and impersonal power. She recalls a passage from Abd al-Hayy Moore's book that Mr. Lundstrom had read in class. Moore wrote that rock gardens help us "see our own natures against the background of earth's organic time-flow."

While these experiences of awareness and insight were satisfying, both Brian and Sarah also feel some dissatisfaction and incompleteness. Brian draws their attention back to the session of zazen.

"You know, while I was meditating I wouldn't have said I was enjoying myself, but when the time was over, I was sorry to see it come to an end."

Sarah nods in agreement. "That's what I felt, too. I wanted to go back into it, even though I wanted it to be over while it was going on."

"This is a good example of the Second Noble Truth of Buddhism," says Mr. Lundstrom. "Suffering is caused by desire, because desire is never satisfied with life as it is. We want out of things we later look back on as enjoyable, and can't really enjoy them later because they're gone.

"Some Buddhists would challenge me on this," Mr. Lundstrom goes on, "because this interpretation of the Second Noble Truth implies that Buddhism is a way of learning how to savor and treasure life. Frankly, that interpretation makes a lot of sense to me. But it's important for you to know that some Buddhists would say this is not what Gautama, the founder of Buddhism, meant, and that wanting to better appreciate life is the desire that most needs to be destroyed if we are to escape from suffering. The purists would say that my interpretation is a typical western reading of Buddhism, and reflects the American tendency to make Buddhism into a kind of advanced psychotherapy."

"Either way," responds Brian rather sadly, "sitting zazen certainly has been a humbling experience. I actually felt that I knew something about Buddhism before I came here today."

"And I feel that anyone who can do this on a regular basis has to be a religious Hercules," Sarah joins in. "Sitting is really hard."

"Don't sell yourselves short, or minimize your experience, or think that there is some reality out there to be attained that is different from what you already know," cautions Mr. Lundstrom. "It's true, there is a kind of spiritual athleticism about Zen, and people who sit often go through a lot of pain in their quest for enlightenment. But there's an equally important tradition within Zen of making fun of such quests, and of people who take their own practice of Zen too seriously. Think of Han-shan, the Chinese poet who laughed uproariously at the self-importance and fussiness of his fellow Buddhists. Think of the Zen master who burned a wooden statue of the Buddha to keep warm during meditation, and the irreverence so many other Zen masters expressed in their efforts to get their students to see around their own egos, and relinquish their attachment to lofty expectations about spiritual truth. Don't forget that famous old piece of advice, 'If you see the Buddha on the road, kill him!'

"I think you both did a fine job today, and commend you for pursuing the logic of the Zen belief that wisdom comes through practice and discipline. If you felt pain when you were sitting," Mr. Lundstrom goes on, "there's nothing inappropriate or spiritually inadequate about that! After all, life *is* suffering," he concludes, referring to the First Noble Truth of Buddhism. All three laugh at the irony of making this discovery a source of congratulation.

Buddhism began in India in the fifth century before the common era. The founder of Buddhism, Siddhartha Gautama, is also known as Shakyamuni Buddha, or the sage of the Shakya clan. Prompted by the realization that old age, sickness, and death were an inevitable part of life, Shakyamuni abandoned his royal family and fortune to take up the life of a wandering ascetic. But after nearly starving himself to death, he found that deprivation brought him no closer to peace or truth. Meditating with a satisfied stomach under the famous Bo tree, he attained enlightenment. He then took up "the middle path," and taught mindfulness in every aspect of life, awareness of suffering, and meditation as a means to enlightenment.

After Shakyamuni's death, Buddhism became the dominant religion in many parts of India, and spread to various parts of Southeast Asia, China, Korea, Japan, Tibet, and Indonesia. A form of Chinese Buddhism known as Ch'an reached Japan in the sixth century of the common era, and after fourteen centuries of development in Japan as Zen, reached the United States and other parts of the Western world.

In India, Vedanta developed in reaction against the atheism of Buddhist philosophy and against Buddhism's rejection of Brahmanism. Thus Vedantists emphasized the ultimate and essential spiritual reality of the impersonal self within each living being, and respect for Brahmanic scriptures that supported this belief, against Buddhist denials of the existence of any permanent spiritual reality, and against Buddhist insistence that the self is nothing more than a construct of consciousness.

Followers of the oldest form of Buddhism, known as *Theravada,* or tradition of the elders, believe that enlightenment is a state of transcendence separate from ordinary consciousness. Theravada Buddhism spread from India to Ceylon (now Sri Lanka) around 250 B.C.E. and then eastward, contributing to the formation of cultural and national identities in many parts of Southeast Asia, including Cambodia, Laos, Burma, and Thailand. The training of Theravadin monks and nuns focuses on the importance of letting go of all forms of desire. European and American students of this tradition are often the first to criticize the western tendency to make Buddhism a means to happier living in this world.

In some contrast, there is less emphasis on the transcendence of enlightenment, and more emphasis on the relativism of all things, including enlightenment, in the *Mahayana,* or Great Vehicle tradition of Buddhism, which spread from India to China and Tibet, and from China to Korea and Japan. The Mahayana emphasis on the relativism of all things is expressed through the concept of nonduality — matter is not separate from mind, light is not separate from dark, life is not separate from death, being is not separate from nonbeing, enlightenment is not separate from ordinary living. One of the early Mahayana texts that became important in the development of Zen is the *Prajnaparamita,* or Perfection of Wisdom, which describes enlightenment as the realization that "form is emptiness, and emptiness is form." In this text, nonduality is expressed through the concept of *sunyata,* or emptiness, and its equation with *prajna,* or wisdom, truth, and ultimate reality. In China and Japan, sunyata has often been rendered in spare ink drawings in which empty space is as much a part of the picture as its lines. In psychological terms, sunyata has often been interpreted to mean that human thought and action is rooted in nothing but the flow of consciousness. As the Ch'an Master Kiangsi Tao-I put it, "The mind is the Buddha."

A second important characteristic of Mahayana traditions is concern for compassion. This concern is expressed in a missionary impulse to alleviate suffering through the spread of Buddhism, and in the idea of *bodhisattvas*, those individuals who choose to postpone their enlightenment in order to help free others from suffering and desire. This concern for compassion is closely tied to the concept of nonduality. In Mahayana worldviews, enlightenment does not really exist as a state of being, or as a state of mind beyond ordinary consciousness. It is awareness of what is. And if what is, is suffering, a person in the process of becoming enlightened cannot stop attending to suffering.

The Ch'an and Zen traditions are distinctive in their emphasis on the logic-defying nature of enlightenment, and on the enlightenment experience as a leap, or instantaneous breakthrough of insight. These traditions are also characterized by an emphatic focus on the transmission of insight from teacher to student. While the student-teacher relationship is important in many forms of Buddhism, in Zen it is set above and apart from the study and veneration of religious texts. Zen teachers belong to particular lineages of spiritual descent and transmit insight to their students through supervision of their meditation. This supervision often revolves around the use of *koans*, or enigmatic questions that teachers give their students to meditate on. One of the most frequently used beginner koans is, "What is *Mu*?" A literal translation of *mu* is "nothing."

In the United States, Zen has developed in new ways in response to the egalitarianism and informality of American culture. Zen practitioners in the United States have softened the authoritarian and hierarchical nature of Japanese Zen. Some have challenged the institutionalization of male dominance within Zen, and worked to bring female leadership and feminist philosophy into American zendos. While Japanese Zen centers around monasteries and the rigid discipline of monastic life, Zen in the United States is predominantly a lay movement. The concept of "Everyday Zen" has taken hold, and centers on the application of Zen attitudes to ordinary living.

In their conversation over green tea, Ned Lundstrom and his students get involved in a discussion about the relationship between Buddhist attitudes toward suffering and those of other religions. In Buddhism, according to the Noble Truths attributed to Shakyamuni, life is suffering, suffering is caused by desire, and the practice of mindfulness in all aspects of life leads to the cessation of desire. In Mahayana Buddhism, compassionate response to suffering involves a missionary impulse to spread Buddhist insight, and the practical means for attaining insight, throughout the world. This missionary impulse, combined with the Buddhist attention to suffering and concern for compassion, strikes Brian as similar to Christianity.

"Buddhism is like Christianity!" says Brian, breaking into the conversation with some excitement. "Christ is the Great Physician, is he not? Christianity focuses on suffering no less than Buddhism," he adds, "and charity, the fundamental Christian virtue, does not seem all that different from Buddhist compassion."

"But Brian," interrupts Sarah somewhat playfully, "doesn't Christianity *recommend* suffering as a means to salvation? Maybe I don't really understand Christianity because I was raised as a Jew, but Jews and Christians both seem really *into* suffering, whereas Buddhists are trying to get out. Think of all those medieval saints, whipping and starving themselves and wearing hair shirts."

"Seriously," Sarah goes on, "there is a lot of suffering to bear if you're a Jew. As someone whose great-aunts and uncles died in the Holocaust, I have the horror of Hitler's death camps and gas chambers seared into my being, and I have been taught to feel responsible for trying to make the world a place where my own children and grandchildren will not be persecuted as their ancestors were."

"So as a Jew," Mr. Lundstrom comments, "you are also looking for a way to end suffering."

"Yes, that's true," acknowledges Sarah, "but I also want to hold onto the suffering of the Jews because it's part of my history and my identity as a human being. It's also part of the world's history that everyone should remember."

"I think you could say something similar about being a Christian," says Brian after a moment. "In Christianity, the way to salvation is through suffering, and through belief in the redemption brought about through Christ's suffering. In Christianity, compassion for others grows out of suffering rather than in freedom from it."

"I see what you are saying," says Mr. Lundstrom thoughtfully. "But I wonder if you can really be compassionate to others if you are holding onto your own suffering. Perhaps there's a common insight in Buddhism and Christianity that suffering is at the core of life, and that the purpose of religion is to attend to it. But I'd like to hear more about how you think the *practice* of Christianity and Judaism compares with Zen meditation, and especially with zazen. Everything about Zen revolves around the practice of meditation, and I wonder if there is anything comparable in Christianity and Judaism?"

"Well, the Eucharist is certainly central to Roman Catholicism," says Brian. "I know that, as a Catholic, participation in the ritual of the Eucharist leads to an experience of the presence of God that affects the way you see everything, at least it's supposed to. This might be similar to the Zen idea that meditation can reveal something about the ultimate nature of reality, and this revelation changes the rest of your life. It would be interesting," he goes on after a pause, "to compare this Catholic sense of the presence of Christ in the Eucharist with the experience of kensho in Zen. At first, the two seem almost opposite — in kensho, emptiness rules, whereas in the Eucharist the presence of Christ fills everything. But if you take the Buddhist perspective, and see mind or consciousness as ultimate reality, then the experience of freedom, joy, and compassion in kensho may not be all that different from the grace that Catholics experience in the Eucharist. But," he adds after a pause, "the Zen emphasis on instantaneous breakthrough does seem different, as does the whole Buddhist rejection of a supreme or universal being like the biblical God or the Hindu Brahma."

"I see a real similarity between Zen meditation and Jewish practice," says Sarah, taking her turn at answering Mr.

Lundstrom's question. "The whole purpose of observing religious law, for the Jew, is to become aware of the presence of God in every part of life. Maybe not all observant Jews actually experience ritual that way, but I think it's the ideal. And isn't this ideal similar, at some level, to the Zen attitude toward flower arranging, rock gardening, and manual labor?"

"That's interesting," muses Mr. Lundstrom. "I wonder if we could go a step further and say that the awareness of dependence on God that is cultivated in Jewish observance might bear some similarity to the concentration on the conditioned nature of existence in Buddhist meditation?"

"So that the observant Jew feels the conditionedness of her existence, and learns to see around her ego, by her participation in Jewish observance. That makes sense, Mr. Lundstrom," says Sarah, "but I'm not sure it works the other way. I mean, the purpose of Zen is not the realization that one depends on God, which is the case in Judaism."

"Good point," concedes Mr. Lundstrom. "I would only trim that difference a bit by saying that if mind takes the place of God in Zen, some similarly respectful attitudes toward life flow out of both forms of devotion. For example, Jews and Buddhists can both be quite self-conscious about what they eat because of their respect for living things."

"Couldn't the point about awareness of one's conditionedness apply to other religions as well?" interrupts Brian. "For example, isn't awareness of one's impermanence and dependence just as crucial to ritual experience in Islam? I think of Islamic prayer and how it is supposed to make a person aware of finitude and dependence on God. At the same time, Sarah's point about the difference between Zen and Judaism could also be made about Zen and Islam—while the Buddhist emphasis on conditionedness might be compatible with the Islamic view of human finitude, the Islamic insistence on human dependence on God does not hold true for Buddhism."

"And if you go back to the Mahayana concept of nondualism at the root of this idea of conditionedness," Sarah adds, "I think you would have to admit that this is more than awareness of one's finitude, or dependence on other living beings. As you were saying earlier, Mr. Lundstrom, nondualism really centers on the idea that being and nonbeing are inseparable. Isn't this right?"

"Yes, it is right," Mr. Lundstrom agrees. "I guess I have to admit that my efforts to draw out similarities among different religions can only be taken so far, and that important points of difference finally stand out more prominently than threads of commonality. However," he adds, unwilling to capitulate completely, "those threads of commonality are no less important for being subtle and often overshadowed. If we're all going to live in the same world together and actually understand something about each other's religious practices and beliefs, then awareness of some of these commonalities may be useful."

"Touché, Professor," says Sarah, smiling. Then, glancing at the clock on wall, she begins to gather herself together in preparation for leaving. "This has really been a great discussion. And thanks for tea."

"And for the zazen, too," says Brian. "I learned a lot. But before we go, I have one more puzzle for you both. I want to hear your reactions to a comparison between zazen and Native American rituals. I know there are a lot of different Native American rituals, but I was thinking specifically about Navajo sandpainting. Because of the special lecture put on by the Religion department earlier this semester," he adds.

"Wow," says Sarah. "It seems really remote. But I wonder. . . . Yes! Isn't sandpainting always a response to some crisis—a misfortune, a sickness—some kind of *suffering*."

"Yes," adds Mr. Lundstrom, becoming excited, "and here we can go a bit further with the Buddhist notion of conditionedness as a point of comparison. In the Navajo world, thought is the basis of all reality. Like Buddhists, the Navajo are very concerned about the events and forms of the material world, while at the same time understanding those events and forms as expressions of thought, or what a Buddhist might call mind."

"But what about nonduality?" asks Sarah. "That doesn't really translate into Navajo ceremony, does it?"

"Well, not exactly, I agree," responds Mr. Lundstrom, "although the Navajo have a strong sense of the contingency of the material world. And their belief in the importance of ceremony for maintaining the harmony of the world is an expression of their belief in the power that death and evil have to unravel this harmony. Given this sense of the dynamic tension between being and nonbeing, I wonder if the Mahayana concept of nonduality is really so far afield. But it's getting late, and I'm not going to give you another opportunity to demonstrate the superiority of your minds."

They all laugh and stand up. Shaking hands with their host, Brian and Sarah say their goodnights and walk back to campus.

SUGGESTIONS FOR FURTHER READING

Chang Chung-Yuan, ed., *Original Teachings of Ch'an Buddhism*, selected from *The Transmission of the Lamp* (New York: Vintage Books, 1971).

Philip Kapleau, *The Three Pillars of Zen: Teaching, Practice, Enlightenment* (New York: Doubleday/Anchor, 1989; orig. 1965).

Abd al-Hayy Moore, *Zen Rock Gardening* (Philadelphia: Running Press, 1992).

Noble Ross Reat, *Buddhism: A History* (Berkeley: Asian Humanities Press, 1994).

John Snelling, *The Buddhist Handbook: A Complete Guide to Buddhist Schools, Teaching, Practice, and History* (Rochester, Vermont: Inner Traditions International, 1991).

Shunryu Suzuki, *Zen Mind, Beginner's Mind: Informal Talks on Zen Meditation and Practice*, ed. Trudy Dixon (New York: Weatherhill, 1970).

A. K. Warder, *Indian Buddhism* (Delhi: Motilal Banarsidass, 1970).

Part II

—🙾—

Experience

Religious experience is the most essential aspect of religion in the sense that without it, religion would be empty, abstract, and meaningless. At the same time, it is the aspect of religion that is most elusive and difficult to describe.

Religious experiences are apprehensions of the sacred. They occur in the consciousness of individuals, and often involve intense states of feeling. These events can have transformative effects on the lives of individuals, and function as guides for thought and behavior. In the preceding section, we saw that religious experience is really the goal of religious practice. That is, people are drawn to ritual and other forms of religious activity because they facilitate immediate and personal experience of what is most important, beautiful, and sacred. In this section we look into the matter of religious experience more deeply.

Also in this section, we consider branches of each of the six traditions that are different from those we considered in the first section. Here Lakota self-sacrifice stands as the example of Native American religious experience, Presbyterian grace represents Christian experience, Jewish mysticism exemplifies Jewish experience, an experience of jihad represents Islam, recognition of God in the Bhagavadgita represents Hinduism, and Tibetan-style awareness of enlightened beings exemplifies Buddhism.

In each of the religious experiences described in this section, religious community figures importantly. Religious experiences draw from the history, teachings, stories, and rituals of the communities in which they occur. Religious experiences also contribute to the life of religious communities, stimulating community outreach as well as enthusiasm for community membership among insiders.

7

Lakota Self-Sacrifice

In the soft light of early morning on the last day of July, with the last pink of dawn still visible in her rearview mirror, Cinda Stevens drives west on Interstate 90 in South Dakota toward the Pine Ridge Indian Reservation, the home of the *Oglala Sioux*, the largest subdivision of the western, or Teton, Sioux. Cinda is a nursing student, born and raised in a Midwestern city far from Pine Ridge. Although she has never been in contact with any Pine Ridge relatives, her mother's grandfather was born on the reservation. Hoping to meet some relatives, and to learn more about their religion, Cinda has decided to visit the annual Pine Ridge *sun dance*, a Plains Indian ceremony of spiritual and cultural renewal.

The sun dance originated in the eighteenth century, probably among the Cheyenne, and spread to other Plains tribes as a major ceremonial event drawing various populations together for feasting, courtship, religious purification, and ordeals designed to infuse hunters and warriors with experiences of spiritual power. Although it may have continued on in some form in secret, the sun dance in its full form died out among the western Sioux after it was banned in 1881 by the U.S. government as part of its efforts to destroy the "savage" customs of the Sioux and persuade them to accept western culture. But it was reborn in modified form on the reservations, where it emerged publicly after 1934, when the government ban against it was partially lifted. No longer a ritual instigated by hunters and warriors seeking power for future conquests, or seeking to repay the spirits for conquests already made, the sun dance became a ritual of spiritual renewal that helped the Sioux retain their cultural identity and endure the hardships of reservation life.

Along with the Brule, Hunkpapa, Mnikowojus, and other subdivisions of the western Sioux, the Oglala are often called *Lakota*, which is the name of their language. The Lakota are well known for their resistance to the U.S. Army and to the encroachment of western culture onto the northern plains during the nineteenth century. Today's Lakota descend from the tribes of the Hunkpapa Chief Sitting Bull, who led the Sioux war of resistance in the 1860s and 1870s, and the legendary Oglala warrior and holy man Crazy Horse, who joined Sitting Bull in defeating General George Armstrong Custer in 1876, killing nearly his entire force at the Battle of Little Bighorn. After this defeat, the U.S. Army conquered the Lakota, killing many, including Sitting Bull and Crazy Horse. The Lakota were forced to relinquish most of their lands, give up their traditional occupations of hunting and warfare, and accept dependence on insufficient rations from the U.S. government.

In an attempt to reverse this desperate situation at the end of the nineteenth century, many Lakota embraced the *ghost dance*, a religious movement promising a supernatural transformation of life on earth, in which the broken and violated world the Lakota had come to inhabit would be rolled away, and the abundant world of the past, with its deceased inhabitants, rolled back in. The ghost dance began among the Paiute Indians of Nevada and swept through a number of western tribes stricken by disease, poverty, and the destruction of their life-ways. Enthusiasm for the ghost dance declined swiftly among the Lakota after 1890, when U.S. soldiers massacred more than two hundred men, women, and children in Big Foot's Mnikowojus band at Wounded Knee Creek. Some of the men were wearing ghost shirts, painted with sacred emblems and figures, believed to protect the wearer from bullets. U.S. Army officers regarded these shirts as military provocations.

While forced to abandon their nomadic life as hunters and severely punished for their reputation as warriors, the Lakota retained important elements of their religion, including their spiritual concepts of war and warriors. Other traditional elements that persist in Lakota religion today include belief in *Wakan Tanka*, the creator God on high who is also a universal spiritual presence encompassing more than four hundred spirits in the Lakota pantheon, and belief in the importance of vision quests and similar forms of religious experience that establish personal relationships between individuals and spirits who bestow power on them. The Lakota also preserve commitment to the gifts believed to be brought to their people by the legendary White Buffalo Cow Woman as a means of communicating with the spirit world, especially the gifts of the sacred pipe, the sweat lodge, and the sun dance.

Since most of the Lakota are Christian (three-fourths of Pine Ridge residents are Catholic or Episcopal), the traditional elements of Lakota religion coexist with Christian belief and experience, and often blend together. Thus Wakan Tanka and the creator God described in the Bible are often understood to be one and the same, and Christian ideas about the redemptive power of Jesus's suffering confirm the traditional Lakota belief that self-sacrifice can be a means of gaining access to the spirit world. Both Christian clerics and traditional holy men have encouraged linkages between Christianity and Lakota religion, although the clerics tend to view Lakota religion as a preparation for Christianity, while the holy men assume the reverse.

In the 1970s, leaders of the leftist American Indian Movement (AIM) turned to the Oglala Sun Dance Chief Frank Fools Crow and to the life story of the Oglala holy man Black

Elk for spiritual instruction. As the religious education of AIM members deepened, the sun dance became increasingly popular among these and other urban Indians, as well as among tourists, and religious seekers looking to Lakota religion for inspiration. The sun dance has grown to accommodate this larger sphere of interested people, and now functions as a means of initiation into Lakota spirituality for those on the periphery of the culture, as well as an experience of spiritual renewal and means of affirming and developing Lakota religion for insiders. The sun dance is one of the most prominent expressions of Lakota religion today. Led by men at campsites both on and off the reservations, sun dances attract thousands of spectators each year, and dozens of individuals pledging to participate in traditional ordeals of self-sacrifice.

Like many of her New Age friends, Cinda is interested in Lakota spirituality because of its respect for the environment, and because it seems to offer an alternative to the consumerism, greed, and materialism that she believes are characteristic of American culture. In her view, the Lakota still represent a tradition of spiritual resistance to American culture, even if its military aspect has diminished. Cinda also feels a strong pull toward the people at Pine Ridge because she is a person with some Oglala blood, and she is eager to find the spiritual roots of her mother's people, and to sink some spiritual roots of her own in alongside.

With these somewhat romantic expectations, Cinda is not fully prepared for either the poverty or the commercialism she encounters when she leaves the Interstate and drives onto the reservation for the first time. She sees dilapidated homes, rusted-out cars, worn clothes, and a number of shops that look to her like tourist traps selling cheap pipes, fake headdresses, candy, and film.

"I don't know what I expected to find," she says aloud, chiding herself for being disappointed. "I guess I was looking for a Garden of Eden. An idyllic village scene with paint horses and a sparkling stream. Something out of a movie about Indians in the nineteenth century."

Following directions obtained at the Pine Ridge Visitor's Center, Cinda finds the campsite where the sun dance is being held. It is the second day of the four-day dance, and the campsite is crowded with people, cars, and innumerable tents set up in a large circle almost a quarter mile in diameter. Cinda parks her car and walks toward the tents, intent on observing as much as she can, and also on finding someone she can talk to, someone who will help guide her toward a real experience of Lakota spirituality.

As Cinda remembers from Fools Crow's account, the sun dance camp involves several concentric areas. The outer circle is comprised of tents and booths, where spectators eat, sleep, and visit, and where food and crafts are sold. Inside that circle are the sweat lodges and preparation tents, where pledgers stay during the four days of the sun dance, praying, fasting, resting, and receiving instruction. This middle circle also includes an open area through which the dancers pass on their way to the innermost circle, and through which spectators pass on their way to the shade arbor encircling the innermost area. The inner "mystery circle," as it is called, is considered sacred ground, and no one is allowed to enter without permission of the sun dance leaders.

In the center of the mystery circle stands the sacred tree. It was "killed" the day before the sun dance began in a ceremony symbolizing the suspension of ordinary growth and the establishment of a four-day hiatus in ordinary time in which spiritual transformation and renewal can occur. Carefully selected from a stand of forty- to fifty-foot cottonwoods, the tree has been blessed by the sun dance chief, chopped once on each of four sides by a young woman believed to be a virgin, and then cut down by several men and trucked to the sun dance campsite. With thanks to Grandmother Earth for producing it, the tree has been stripped of its lower leaves, planted in a hole in the center of the ceremonial space where the sun dance chief has deposited flesh offerings from his own body, and then hung with pouches of tobacco for the spirits, colored flags representing the spirits of the cardinal directions, and doll-like representations of a holy man and a buffalo that may inspire visions in those who dance. As the focus of the dancers' religious experiences, the tree creates a sacred world in which power seems to flow between spirits and dancers, and between the dancers who communicate with the spirits and the people.

After inspecting the sacred tree from the shade arbor, Cinda watches the pledgers dancing in the hot sun for more than an hour. Later, she returns to the tent area, stopping at a booth where a middle-aged woman selling leather goods is working on a small fringed bag. The woman looks up in a friendly way, and Cinda plunges in.

"I'm sorry to interrupt you," Cinda says, "but I wonder if you could tell me where I could find out something about Lakota spirituality." Surprised by such a blunt request, the woman draws back a few inches and looks at Cinda quizzically, and somewhat dubiously. If outsiders come to the sun dance to be initiated into Lakota spirituality, they do not succeed easily, or without proving themselves worthy.

"My great-grandfather was an Oglala from Pine Ridge," Cinda adds quickly, hoping to avoid the woman's dismissal.

"Oh, well, then," says the woman, her smile returning. "Perhaps you have some relatives here. What was your grandfather's name?"

The two discuss names and families for a while, and Cinda repeats some of the things her mother has told her about her great-grandfather. The woman directs Cinda to a group of tents across the circle, and suggests that she introduce herself there.

"They might be related to your family," the woman says. "One of the men over there will be pierced tomorrow. And one of the women may give a flesh offering. They might help you find some of the experience you are looking for."

Thanking the woman for her help, Cinda moves away, ruminating about the possibility of meeting lost relatives, and apprehensive about suddenly coming close to people whose religious beliefs were leading them to inflict deliberate and considerable pain on themselves. Uneasy, but intensely interested, she resolves to find out more about the religious experiences sought by the pledgers.

Walking around the circle to the cluster of tents the woman selling bags had described, Cinda approaches a man who looks like he might be in his seventies, sitting on a camp stool in front of one of the tents, smoking a hand-rolled cigarette, apparently deep in thought. Stopping a few yards away, she clears her throat, says hello, and explains that she is looking for some relatives. He looks her in the eyes for a moment, and then calls into the tent in Lakota. A small boy comes out, followed by his mother and grandmother, who greet Cinda politely. Another stool and some chairs appear, and they all sit together for a while, figuring out Cinda's relationship, pointing out the tents of other relatives around the circle, and telling stories about those who are gone.

"It is good that you have come during the summer for a sun dance," the man says after a while, "because the sun dance is traditionally the time when members of the same band come together and join other bands and other tribes. It is a time when the people get together, and the relatives come home."

Happy at being so warmly included, Cinda describes her desire for a firsthand experience of Oglala spirituality. "I know that I'm just a beginner," she confesses, "and that you have spent your lives in touch with the spirits and the reality they represent. And I know I have missed out on a lot, in terms of being trained and prepared for a real experience of the spirits. But I would like to go back with something to remember, something I can call on, and build on."

"There is a lot for you to learn, and you will need to be patient," the man responds. "The holy men will have to teach you. And the women will have to teach you. You will have to come back here many times to participate in the ceremonies, to learn from the people, and work with them.

"One more thing I will tell you," he says. "To receive power from the spirits, you must purify and humble yourself. You must be ready to cry to the spirits for help."

Having pitched her own small tent among those of her new-found relatives, Cinda is awakened just before dawn the next morning by the camp crier, calling the people to the third day of the sun dance, the day that the piercing will begin. After washing and eating, she and the others arrive in the shade arbor in time to see the pledgers file through the two yellow flags at the eastern door of the mystery circle. Some of the men are carrying pipes filled with sacred tobacco. Many of the men have figures or designs painted on their bodies, and quite a few have red circles painted on their chests indicating the spots where they will be pierced. They move clockwise around the mystery circle, stopping before the sun dance altar, located at the west of the circle, facing the rising sun. After placing their pipes alongside the altar, the pledgers sing, "*Tunkashila*, Grandfather, have pity on us. We have come here and are doing this so that everything will be right with us." The tension among the spectators is palpable, and some of the pledgers' relatives begin to cry, their sobs contributing to the petition to the grandfather spirit to infuse the pledgers, and their people, with spiritual power. One of Cinda's cousins points out his brother Ben, who has pledged to be pierced. Ben hopes to receive power from the spirits so that he can bring strength to his people as an ambulance driver, paramedic, and someday, he hopes, as a religious healer.

Moving to the north and then to the south, the pledgers sing and dance, raising their hands occasionally in appeals to Wakan Tanka or the guiding grandfather spirit Tunkashila, reaching up to touch their spiritual power and feeling it run down through their arms. Many participants in the sun dance believe that this contact with the spirits gives the dancers powers of healing, and at a certain point in the morning, the sun dance chief admits a number of individuals who are sick or injured into the mystery circle to be blessed by the dancers. Through simple acts of touching, the dancers generate hope in these individuals, as well as feelings of being infused with holy power. After the healing blessings have been performed, Ben's older half-sister May asks permission to enter the mystery circle to make a flesh offering.

As a woman, May cannot be pierced. But she can smoke the sacred pipe, purify herself in the women's sweat lodge, receive instruction from the religious leaders of the sun dance, and pray and dance to the spirits, to Grandmother Earth, Tunkashila, and Wakan Tanka. And she can make a flesh offering.

May is inspired to make this self-sacrifice as part of her recovery from alcoholism. She needs help from the spirits to be a good influence on her children and nieces and nephews, and to go back to school so that she can get a good job and be a strong member of her community. And as in the other ordeals of the sun dance, the power May may receive as an individual as a result of her self-sacrifice is not a gift for her alone, but one that will benefit her community. As the older women explain it, the spirits might give power to the people through her.

Now within the mystery circle, May dances and sings, reaching her arm up to Wakan Tanka, and then down to Grandmother Earth. Feeling her weakness and fear like a presence inside her, May wants intensely to focus her life, find direction, and break through her fear. She cries to Wakan Tanka for help and strength. As the sun dance chief directs her to a spot on the ground near the altar, May tunes in on the drums, and allows their sound to fill her consciousness and expand her senses, so that the beat of the drums and the beat of her heart seem to be one, and she feels life in the ground beneath her, holding and lifting her toward the sky.

The chief sits down cross-legged on the ground next to her, takes some grey powdered medicine from a bag, and rubs it on the outside of her upper left arm, where May indicates she wants to take her flesh. He hands her a sharp razor. Using the thumb and index finger on both hands he pinches her skin tightly in two places about two inches apart, raising the skin away from the muscles. With little hesitation, May makes the appropriate cuts and lifts out a small rectangle of skin. The chief rubs more medicine on her wound, takes the piece of flesh she gives him, and places it respectfully in another pouch, where he will keep it until he places it on the altar as a gift to the spirits. As he helps her stand up, May becomes aware of her weakness and then feels it flowing out of her as her body begins to sway. Moved by gratitude, relief, and happiness, she feels a new strength flowing into her body. The drums beating through her, she begins to dance, tears flowing down her cheeks, left arm lifted to the sky.

Later that day, Ben and a dozen other men are pierced. The holy man attending Ben makes two incisions on both sides of his chest, inserts wooden skewers under the skin on either side, and ties ropes to the skewers. Dazed from the piercing, and from two-and-a-half days without food or much water, he gets to his feet slowly, his head bent, his shoulders drooping. He follows his guide, who holds the loose ends of the ropes in his hands, walks closer to the sacred tree, and fixes the ropes in the fork of the tree above their heads. This task completed, the holy man begins blowing an eagle whistle, and Ben lifts his head up and steps backward, pulling against the ropes affixed to his chest, strengthened by the sound of the whistle and the feeling of spiritual power it invokes. Taking up his own eagle whistle, he blows it repeatedly, calling to Tunkashila. The sun shines through the leaves of the sacred tree above him, and through the hoop held by the figure of the holy man hung in the branches, which becomes for Ben a visible expression of the circle of people drawn in union and support around him. He feels exalted and strong. The skewers in his chest break through his skin and he stumbles backward, free.

The next day, other men are pierced for two different ordeals. Several are pierced in both breasts and in the center of the chest and then suspended a foot off the ground from ropes tied to four posts. One of the men dances, shoulders turning and feet stepping in the air as the drums beat and the sun dance chief blows his eagle whistle. Cinda, her relatives, and all the people around them stand transfixed by the man's apparent communication with the spirit world.

Also on the fourth day, several men are pierced and attached with ropes to buffalo skulls. For some spectators, this is the culminating ordeal, and the courageous efforts the pledgers make to break free of the heavy skulls dramatize a common experience of life. Many of the spectators and pledgers have been pulled down by life, and the life of their people has been pulled down by many weights — poverty, unhappiness, bad health, untimely deaths, poor education, and lack of opportunity. The dancers drag the skulls across the ground, and when they weaken visibly, the sun dance chief invites children into the circle, who sit and ride on the skulls, adding weight to help the dancers in their struggle. Amidst encouragement and wailing from all sides, the dancers finally tear free, living symbols of the victory of their people.

As a witness to this culminating act of courage and self-sacrifice, Cinda feels that she, too, has been infused with the power of the spirits. She has also come to feel the strength of the Oglala people. As one who has begun to experience the power of the sun dance for herself, Cinda finds herself identified with the Lakota community and its ongoing effort to survive.

SUGGESTIONS FOR FURTHER READING

Joseph G. Jorgensen, *The Sun Dance Religion: Power for the Powerless* (Chicago: University of Chicago Press, 1974; orig. 1972).

Thomas E. Mails, *Fools Crow* (Lincoln: University of Nebraska Press, 1990; orig. 1979).

Marla N. Powers, *Oglala Women: Myth, Ritual, and Reality* (Chicago: University of Chicago Press, 1986).

William K. Powers, *Oglala Religion* (Lincoln: University of Nebraska Press, 1982; orig. 1975).

James R. Walker, *Lakota Society*, ed. Raymond J. DeMallie (Lincoln: University of Nebraska Press, 1982).

8

Presbyterian Grace

In a Presbyterian church in California, David Kim speaks to a congregation of Korean Americans. He is describing his work as a missionary to Asian street kids, many of whom have run away from home and become involved in drugs and prostitution.

"Not every kid is willing to talk with us. But some are. These kids are starved for care and attention and love. Their talk is obscene and cynical, and they don't trust anyone easily. But their want for love is deep. It is important to make sincere and strenuous efforts to reach these young people. Our love of God demands it.

"I have been reviled on many occasions," David went on. "And the gospel message of Jesus Christ has been reviled. On one occasion recently, several members of a gang cornered me in an alley. One of them spit in my face, saying 'This is what we think of your God Jesus Christ.' They called me foul names, and they called our Lord and Savior foul names. I thought I was going to die in that alley. I thought they were going to stab me and beat me and leave me bleeding to death in that outpost of hell. But at that moment, feeling their rage surround me so closely I could taste it, I felt God draw near. I was not afraid. I was not afraid to die.

"I believe that at that moment," he continued after a pause, "those young men also felt the presence of God. Their rage died down. They met my eyes, and their eyes looked baffled, open, and questioning. They stepped back, and the tension in their bodies relaxed.

"I will say to you honestly that I did not know what to do next. I felt like kneeling down in prayer right there in the alley and offering up thanks to God, but I sensed that this would break the closeness between us and remove me from them. So I just said 'Thanks,' and reached out and firmly shook the leader's hand. I shook hands with the others, too, and we exchanged names. I told them that meeting them had made me very hungry, and we all laughed. I invited them to my apartment for a meal.

"They hesitated. And, I'm ashamed to say it, I hesitated, too. I pictured them in my one-room apartment, fingering my guitar and my books, and wondering how much my little TV would bring on the street. I don't have many things, and I thought that things didn't mean much to me. But I found out in that moment that my fear of losing those things was greater than my love of God. I felt wretched. Again I felt like falling to my knees, this time to beg God's forgiveness. But I felt that would be self-indulgent. And I condemned myself for caring more about myself than about the young men who, in that awful moment of my failure, were watching me intently.

"Once again, God's grace intervened. Another member of the group, a boy named Choon-seo, said, 'I wouldn't let you guys in my apartment either.'

"'What apartment, man?' said one of the others. 'You have no apartment, man. You're just trying to make this guy feel better.'

"'And for that,' I said, feeling redeemed, and thankful, and very happy, 'Choon-seo gets to make the choice between tomato soup or chicken noodle.'

"I can report to you," David went on, addressing the congregation, "that two of the young men I met in the alley that night are back in school, and another is working full-time in a grocery. These three have reestablished contact with their families and enrolled in drug-treatment programs. But Choon-seo is dead. His body, with four bullet holes in it, was found on the ground floor of an abandoned building. His business partners apparently felt he was going to betray them.

"Through your support of this mission, you have helped bring life where there is death and hope where there is hopelessness," David continued after a pause, appealing to the congregation. "This mission needs your continued help and support. We need a halfway house where young people trying to turn their lives around can at least get a night's sleep without worrying that they will be hunted down in the middle of the night by their old gangs. And we really need another missionary. Someone who can work with the young women on the streets. They are more vulnerable to prostitution than the young men and just as vulnerable to drug addiction. They are frequently victims of violence because their pimps and dealers and boyfriends beat them, often routinely. Their self-esteem and dignity as human beings are sunk in despair, and the lives of their children, when the children survive, are pitiful. These young women and their children need help. They are God's children, and the mothers of God's children. Thank you for everything you have done and can do in their behalf. In the name of Jesus Christ, amen."

As the church organ began playing softly and two of the young people from the mission began taking up a special offering for the mission, David climbed down the steps from the pulpit and sat next to the church minister in one of the two seats at the side of the communion table, where the elements of the Eucharist are distributed and money offerings given to the church by congregants are placed. The minister nodded appreciatively, and David could see there were tears in his eyes.

This show of support for his talk did not make David feel any better. In fact, he felt like a hypocrite. He had talked too much about himself and not enough about the people he served. He had made it seem that he had a special relationship with God, and that he was one of God's saints, when, in fact, he was struggling to find God, and probably more distant from God than many of the young people he served. Although many of these youth were angry at God, and swore at God, and even told David that God didn't exist, they knew what faith meant. They knew what redemption and salvation were about, and they could smell a pretender a mile away.

"Wait a minute," David thought, "I'm getting carried away with being down on myself. This self-critical self-absorption is just another form of pride. I did my best today. And the grace of God that I experienced in that alley were real, and important to talk about. I just need to keep trying to do God's will, believe in the reality and power of God's grace, and hope he will forgive me and show me the way back to the path of faith when I fall off."

As the organ moved into the minor chords of the Korean hymn, everyone stood to sing the first and second verses, first in Korean, then in English, as the young people who had passed the collection plates brought the mission offering to the minister at the altar.

> When I had not yet learned of Jesus Christ
> When I refused to listen to God's call,
> I was defiant then, till God broke through;
> Now by God's grace Christ is my all in all.
>
> Whatever talent God has given me
> I pledge to use in service and in love.
> Joined with my God to lift my neighbor's load,
> New strength and hope are given from above.

The Presbyterian Church first emerged in seventeenth-century England and Scotland as a relatively moderate form of Reformed Protestantism. While Presbyterians dissented from the established Church of England and contributed to the overthrow of the English monarchy in 1640, they were far less radical than

Baptists and Quakers, whose emphasis on the authority of individual religious experience led them to reject any form of civil or church government that attempted to control the individual's relationship to God. Unlike these more radical English Protestants, seventeenth-century Presbyterians believed in the necessity of a strong church government that united members of many congregations in a single church and cooperated with state government to maintain a Christian society. But they agreed with more radical Protestants in their hostility to the Roman Catholic Church, and in their commitment to carrying forward the principles of the *Protestant Reformation*. The Reformation was a sixteenth-century religious movement that focused on the central importance of each believer's personal relationship with God, and criticized the Roman Church for its belief in the need for priestly mediation between believers and God.

Roman Catholic concepts of priestly authority have roots in the historical development of the Roman Catholic Church. Christianity began as an offshoot of Judaism, and its members were persecuted by the Roman Empire until the Emperor Constantine made it the religion of the empire in the fourth century. The Christian Church soon divided into a Greek-speaking eastern branch centered in Constantinople and a Latin-speaking western branch centered in Rome. While the imperial government was centered in Constantinople, the Roman branch of the church developed a separate form of government headed by the Pope, a bishop elected to the office of the *vicar*, or representative and chief agent, of Christ on earth, and successor to the disciple Peter, the "rock" on whom Christ is said to have built his church. Under the authority of the papacy, the Roman Catholic Church functioned as the chief sponsor of art and learning in Europe during the medieval period, and as a stabilizing political force. The strength of the church in these areas depended on the strength of the papacy and its control over religious doctrine and church organization.

Sixteenth-century Protestant rejection of Roman Catholic ideas about the church, the papacy, and priestly authority not

Holy people as depicted by the Navajo. The Holy People are the inner forms of natural phenomena. As this picture shows, they are believed to be persons, but not human persons. The Navajo seek blessings and power from the Holy People by representing them and drawing them into sandpaintings. (Photograph courtesy of Christie's Images)

Hubert and/or Jan van Eyck, The Crucifixion; The Last Judgment *(c. 1420–25).* These paintings depict many important elements of Christian belief. *The Crucifixion* shows the suffering and death of Jesus amidst Roman soldiers, Jews, and grieving women. *The Last Judgment* shows the eternal Christ in heaven drawing believers to himself while condemning the wicked to hell. (The Metropolitan Museum of Art, Fletcher Fund, 1933 [33.92.a])

Black Elk. The Oglala Sioux Holy Man, Black Elk, was a leader in revitalizing the Lakota sun dance after the ban against it was lifted by the United States government. On Lakota reservations today, traditional versions of the sun dance follow Black Elk's pattern. (Copyright Smithsonian Institute)

Choir members celebrating the chartering of Capital Korean Church in Sacramento, California. These religious singers are participants in one of the Presbyterian churches in the United States where hymns are sung in both Korean and English and many members of the congregation come from Korean-American families. (*1997 Mission Yearbook for Prayer and Study*, Presbyterian Church)

A practitioner of puja *in India transferring his own life force into the* murti *of his god.* This household shrine is the center of family worship and prayer. Each object in the shrine has special meaning for the individuals who worship there. The statues of gods have gone through a ritual process intended to imbue them with living breath. (Photo: Paul B. Courtright)

A group of Hassidic men. Hasidic Jews are famous for expressing religious joy in dance and song. This joyfulness has often coincided with suffering or grief. The Hasidim in this photo are dancing before the Wailing Wall in Jerusalem, where many Jews come to shed their tears. (Corbis-Bettmann)

Opening of Sura VII of the Qur'an from a fourteenth-century Egyptian illuminated text. This artful rendering of a passage from the Qur'an illustrates the reverence Muslims have for their most holy book. Muslims believe that Allah revealed the Qur'an in Arabic to his prophet Muhammad. Translations of the Qur'an into other languages are not as sacred as the original Arabic revelation. (By permission of the British Library)

A Persian description of the prophet Muhammad's journey to heaven. Pious Muslims show great respect for the prophet Muhammad and model their lives on his life and teachings. However, Muslims do not believe that Muhammad is one with Allah, as Christians believe Jesus Christ is one with God, nor do they pray to him, as Christians pray to Christ.

(By permission of the British Library)

Dome of the Mosque of Shaykh Lutfallah in Isfahan, Iran. This Islamic house of prayer illustrates some of the ways in which religious principles are conveyed through architecture and design. While this mosque conveys a sense of beauty and geometric harmony, it contains no representation of any human or natural form because of the danger of confusing Allah with his creatures. (Photo courtesy of Asian Art Archives, University of Michigan. Photographer: Arthur Upham Pope)

Arjuna and Krishna. This illustration of an episode from the beloved Bhagavadgita shows the warrior Arjuna and his divine charioteer Krishna driving into battle. Arjuna hesitates to face friends and kin in combat, but Krishna counsels him to fulfill his duty valiantly, and with a pure heart. (Philadelphia Museum of Art: Purchased Bell funds)

Hui Neng, the Sixth Ch'an Patriarch, chopping bamboo at the moment of enlightenment. One of the most illustrious figures in Chinese Buddhism, the Sixth Patriarch attains enlightenment not by reading Buddhist scriptures or worshipping at Buddhist shrines, but by performing a mundane task. Note that the energy and simplicity of the drawing conveys something about the quality of enlightenment in the Ch'an and Zen traditions. (Tokyo National Museum)

Tsong Khapa and his disciples receiving insight from Manjushri. This painted cloth shows Manjushri, the god of wisdom, transmitting enlightenment to the great Tibetan philosopher Jay Tsong Khapa. According to Tibetan lore, Manjushri was a perfectly enlightened Buddha in another world ages ago. Note the stylistic similarity of this religious art to the Indian painting of Arjuna and Krishna, and its stylistic difference from the Ch'an drawing of the Sixth Patriarch. (The Newark Museum/Art Resource, NY)

The Dalai Lama. As the fourteenth Dalai Lama, Tenzin Gyatso is the religious and political leader of Tibet who, in exile, has concerned himself with the transmission of his religious tradition to the contemporary world. He is believed to be the recipient of wisdom that descends from Shakyamuni Buddha through Tsong Khapa. (© Alison Wright)

A Jewish family celebrating a Passover seder. Passover is celebrated by Jews all over the world in commemoration of God's freeing the ancient Jews from slavery in Egypt. The central event of this Jewish holiday is a seder, or ritual meal, that includes items of food that are symbolic of the Passover story. (Ted Spiegel/Corbis)

only involved criticism of the abuses of clerical authority in the Roman Catholic Church, but also responsiveness to new devlopments in printing, commercial trade, and humanistic philosophy. Scholars often interpret the Protestant Reformation as a challenge to medieval concepts of government, authority, and philosophy epitomized by the Roman Catholic Church, and as a harbinger of modern society, in which the church's role as the mainstay of social order would be eclipsed by individual conscience, marriage, and nuclear family life. With its strong emphasis on the individual's personal relationship with God, and its accompanying criticism of the Roman Catholic Church's overarching authority and apparent control of the means of grace, the Protestant Reformation represented the emergence of modernity.

During the sixteenth century, debates between Catholic and Protestant churchmen often focused on the sacraments, especially on the Eucharist and the Catholic belief in transubstantiation. As you recall from chapter 2 in the first part of this book, the doctrine of transubstantiation involves the assertion that the essential nature of the bread and wine used in the Eucharist is changed, by infusion of God's redemptive grace, into the body and blood of Christ. Presbyterians and other English and Scottish Protestants objected to the idea that a priest could conduct the infusion of grace into the Eucharist, and to the implication that cucharistic elements would be essentially changed through that ritual act, whether or not the priest, or any of the recipients of the eucharistic meal, actually had faith. English and Scottish Protestants defined grace as faith, still emphasizing the origin of grace in God, but locating its redemptive effect in the relationship between the believer and God. Thus grace occurred not in the Eucharist itself but in the believer's soul, and in its communion with God.

The Westminster Confession, written in 1646, is the standard of Presbyterian doctrine. In its definition of *justification*, God's act of making a believer just, righteous, and acceptable, the confession declares in Chapter XI that faith involves "receiving and resting on Christ and his righteousness," and that faith "is the alone (only) instrument of justification." By contrast, during the Council of Trent during the sixteenth century, the pope, cardinals, and bishops of the Roman Church convened to define Catholic doctrine over against Protestant beliefs. In a "Decree Concerning the Sacraments" issued in 1547 as part of the Council of Trent, the church officially stated that "If anyone says that the sacraments . . . do not contain the grace which they signify, . . . as though they are only outward signs of grace or justice received through faith, . . . let him be anathema."

Of course, emphasis on the power of grace working in the believer's heart had long been central to the spirituality of the Roman Church, and Protestants who denied its importance in Catholic life were simply mistaken. Moreover, the old tensions between Catholics and Protestants have lessened considerably in recent years, and most Catholics today resist simplistic equations between grace and the sacraments of the church. As one Catholic theologian said, "There is no such thing as bottled grace!"

On the other hand, Cathlics do link grace with the sacraments of the church, and Protestant criticism of this linkage has played an important role in shaping the Protestant view that the workings of grace are located instead in the context of interpersonal relationships. David Kim's experience of persons estranged from one another drawing closer and becomeing more trusting of one another can be understood as an expression of this Protestant tendency to define grace in relational terms rather than in terms of the infusion of grace through the official sacraments of the church. While many Catholics do, in fact, discover works of God in encounters and events outside the church, official Catholic doctrine would emphasize that grace, in the sense of an act of God that actually regenerates the soul, flows into individual lives primarily through the church and its sacraments. But David's experience of grace occurred outside church walls in an encounter with young men who were not members of his church, or any church. Of course David hoped this experience would bring them *to* church. In his later work with some of these youth, he encouraged them to become church members, arguing that what they experienced during that encounter on the street was an act of divine love and communion that altered their lives, and made them responsible for becoming church members dedicated to praising God and spreading his love.

David Kim's understanding of Christianity is affected not only by his membership in a church with theological roots in British Protestantism, but also by his Korean background. Since the late-nineteenth century, Presbyterian Christianity has served as a vehicle for expressing national pride and self-determination in Korea. As a small country situated between China and Japan, Korea has, during the course of many centuries, been vulnerable to domination by both of these larger powers. While their country has often been prey to foreign intervention, Koreans have expressed fierce commitment to their own cultural identity. Presbyterian Christianity encouraged this self-reliance through its strong commitment to the authority of individual experience, which is clearly expressed in the Westminster Confession's emphasis on faith.

Beginning in the nineteenth century, Presbyterian missionaries were active in Korea and a significant minority of Koreans converted to Christianity as a result of missionary effort. Since the end of Japanese domination and the division of North and South Korea in 1945, Korean Presbyterians have immigrated to the United States both as refugees from Communist North Korea, where Christianity has been suppressed, and as recipients of U.S. influence in South Korea, where U.S. economic and military support has been significant. Out of a population of more than forty million in South Korea, more than a quarter are Christian, and more than half of these are affiliated with Presbyterian churches. Among Korean immigrants to the United States, membership in the Presbyterian Church is common, although other forms of Christianity, and various forms of Buddhism and folk religion are also represented. Korean Americans make up a growing percentage of Presbyterian students in U.S. theological seminaries, and these students tend to be more religiously conservative than

Presbyterian seminarians from other ethnic backgrounds. Many congregations of Korean Presbyterians exist, and numerous mergers have occurred between Korean and previously established congregations in the United States. The official hymnbook of the Presbyterian Church, U.S.A., the largest Presbyterian denomination in the United States, includes hymns composed by Koreans, with verses in both Korean and English.

While commitment to the Presbyterian Church and to Presbyterian doctrine is as strong among them as among any members of the church, Korean Americans carry cultural and ethnic expectations that add distinctively Korean elements to their experiences of grace. As inheritors of a culture strongly influenced by *Confucianism*, the Chinese court tradition of ritual observance and moral virtue, Korean Americans are more likely than other Americans to appreciate rules for behavior, speech, and thought, and more likely to cultivate highly formal and respectful attitudes toward persons in authority, and to treat older persons with veneration. The orderliness, formality, and deferential respect prized in Korean culture may lend an additional element of self-control to the religious experiences of Korean American members of the Presbyterian Church, which is a branch of Protestant Christianity where highly demonstrative expressions of religious experience are more infrequent than not.

While Korean Presbyterianism carries some of this Confucian influence on Korean culture, it also carries elements of Mahayana Buddhism. Buddhism reached Korea through China in the fourth century of the common era, and flourished as the state religion of Korea until suppressed by Confucianism in the sixteenth century. The Presbyterian concern for experiences of personal transformation and outreach to others coincides with the compassion for suffering in Mahayana Buddhism, as well as with Buddhism's quest for enlightenment. These Buddhist concerns have shaped Korean culture over the centuries, and contributed to Christianity's appeal to Koreans.

As it developed in Korea, Buddhism built on and consolidated indigenous tribal religions led by *shamans,* or religious specialists who entered trance states at will to communicate with spirits for the purpose of healing and *divination,* or discovering hidden knowledge and seeing into the future. Buddhist monks in Korea often functioned like shamans, and both ruling elites and common people turned to them for protection, power, and national identity. The bureaucratic rituals and moral codes of Confucianism developed alongside this Buddhist shamanism and eclipsed Buddhist authority between the late 1500s and 1910, when Japan took over Korea and imposed Japanese forms of Buddhism. This imposition of foreign variants of Buddhism triggered a nationalistic revival of *Son* Buddhism, the indigenous Korean version of the Ch'an or Zen tradition. Since 1945, numerous Buddhist sects have flourished in South Korea, and among South Koreans who claim affiliation with an institutionalized form of religion, about half are Buddhist and half are Christian.

Attention to suffering and compassion is strong in both Christianity and Buddhism, but important differences exist with respect to attitudes toward the relationship between suffering and enlightenment or redemption. While Buddhists believe that enlightenment is a release from suffering and is attained through relinquishment of the desires that cause suffering, Christians believe that redemption, the Christian counterpart to Buddhist enlightenment, comes through suffering. Christians believe that suffering is a necessary ingredient in redemptive change, and that the experience of grace is not so much a release from suffering (as enlightenment is in Buddhism) as it is a way of bearing suffering and translating its meaning into positive, redemptive terms.

Christians have often connected suffering with the experience of *self-sacrifice.* This experience is exemplified by the sufferings of Jesus, whom Christians believe to be the *Christ,* the Son of God and Savior of humankind. In Christian belief, Jesus willingly accepted betrayal, humiliation, and crucifixion as a kind of gift or payment to God for the sins of others, and as a means of obtaining God's grace for them. Thus in Christianity, grace is obtained through suffering, and self-sacrifice is a means of emulating Christ and his willingness to bear suffering. In Presbyterianism and other forms of Protestant Christianity, special emphasis is also placed on the power that the example of self-sacrifice can have in bringing grace to others. While maintaining that grace always comes from God, Presbyterians also believe that individuals can represent this grace to others through relationships of love, forgiveness, and self-sacrifice.

This aspect of Christianity can be compared with Lakota experiences of self-sacrifice. In the Lakota sun dance, self-sacrifice is an offering to the spirits, a means of petitioning the spirits for power, and a way of preparing oneself to receive spiritual power. In the belief that one has nothing more valuable to give than one's own body, Lakota sun dancers give flesh offerings and undergo bodily piercings to honor the spirits and receive their power. As we have seen in the previous chapter, many Lakota participants in the sun dance are also members of Christian churches, and belief in the compatibility of Christianity and Lakota religion is widespread among the Lakota people. In both traditions, experiences of spiritual power are central, and self-sacrifice is respected as a vehicle to those experiences.

Some important distinctions can also be drawn. Christian experiences of grace focus more narrowly and exclusively on a very specific form of divine reality, namely Jesus Christ, while Lakota experiences of divine power are tied to a variety of different spirits. The Catholic emphasis on the infusion of grace in the Eucharist corresponds to the Lakota understanding of the infusion of spiritual power in sun dance participants, and this correspondence is something that Lakota people with Catholic backgrounds are quite aware of and articulate about. But at the same time, the highly structured administration of the sacraments in the Catholic Church can be contrasted with the highly personalized management of spiritual power in Lakota religion. Lakota sun dancers would agree with Presbyterians that the experience of divine reality is completely dependent on the state of the believer's heart.

As we have seen, the Presbyterian emphasis on the importance of the individual and the integrity of individual experience has played a role in Korean history as a means of mediating cultural identity and pride. In this respect, Presbyterian experiences of grace have served to strengthen Korean commitment to cultural community in something of the same way that Lakota experiences of self-sacrifice have served to strengthen Lakota community. But while in both cases there is a strong concern for building community through religious experience, the Presbyterian concept of community is not defined by kinship and ethnicity to the same degree as the Lakota concept. However conservative Korean Presbyterians may be in their adherence to Korean culture, they understand Christianity as a universal religion intended for people of every ethnic group. A stronger degree of religious universalism among Korean Presbyterians leads this group to place less emphasis than Lakota sun dancers on the relationship between religious and ethnic experience.

SUGGESTIONS FOR FURTHER READING

Randall Herbert Balmer, *The Presbyterians* (Westport: Greenwood Press, 1993).

Milton J. Coalter and Virgil Cruz, eds., *How Shall We Witness?: Faithful Evangelism in a Reformed Tradition* (Louisville: John Knox Press, 1995).

James Huntley Grayson, *Korea: A Religious History* (Oxford: Clarendon Press, 1989).

John H. Leith, ed., *Creeds of the Churches: A Reader in Christian Doctrine from the Bible to the Present* (Atlanta: John Knox Press, 1982; orig. 1963).

Noble Ross Reat, "The Development of Buddhism in Korea," *Buddhism: A History* (Berkeley: Asian Humanities Press, 1994), 165-185.

Kenneth R. Ross, *Presbyterian Theology and Participatory Democracy* (Edinburgh: Church of Scotland Board of Women's Missions and Unity by St. Andrew Press, 1993).

H. J. Schroeder, trans., *The Canons and Decrees of the Council of Trent,* (Rockford, IL: Tan Books and Publishers, 1978; orig. 1941).

Chai-shin Yu and R. Guisso, eds., *Shamanism: The Spirit World of Korea* (Berkeley: Asian Humanities Press, 1988).

9

Jewish Mysticism

Sarah's parents were stunned when she told them she wanted to attend Jewish Theological Seminary in New York City to study to become a rabbi.

"A rabbi!" Her mother could not contain her astonishment. "A rabbi! But Sarah," her mother said after a moment, "are you sure you want to spend seven years in seminary? It's a long and extremely specialized form of graduate study. What if you change your mind three years in, or the year before you finish?"

"I guess that's a risk I'd have to take," responded Sarah. "It's the same kind of time frame for someone working to become a professor or a physician. And besides, it's what I really want to do. The wonderful experiences I've had studying Judaism and interacting with other Jews this year at school have really centered my life and given me a sense of direction and purpose. By becoming a rabbi I could fill my life with experiences like these. I could also learn more about how Jews throughout history have understood God. I could take more responsibility for interpreting that history and for carrying it forward. And I

could help others learn to experience God and develop loyalty to Judaism. If I don't dedicate myself to this now, I'll
always feel that I missed out on what I wanted to do, and never
gave myself the chance to become the person I dreamed of
becoming."

"But Sarah," her mother repeated, concerned that her
daughter seemed suddenly to have grown so different, and
wanting to catch up with her, "where did you get this dream?
We don't have any rabbis in our family. We don't even know
any rabbis well enough to understand what a rabbi's life is
really like."

"Actually, I met several rabbis at school whose learning and
devotion to God I admired. At *Hillel*, the Jewish organization
on campus, Rabbi Schneiderman was great, and I talked with
him a lot about what I was thinking and feeling. We had some
visiting speakers who talked about the changes in Judaism in
the United States today, the difference that it makes to have
women rabbis in some congregations, the relationship
between Jewish spirituality and the ecology movement, the
contributions Jews have made to science and social welfare,
and the fascinating world of Jewish *mysticism*. (Mysticism is an
old tradition within Judaism, centered on immediate experience of God and discovery of God's nature.) It's Jewish mysticism that really inspires me, Mom," Sarah explained. "I've
been thinking a lot about the relationship between Jewish
mysticism and real life, and about the renewal of Jewish mysticism in the world today, and its potential for inspiring social
action and change."

"You're going to have to teach me about Jewish mysticism,"
said her mother. "And about the relationship between it and
social action. I thought mystics were not interested in politics
or in social change."

"Well, in some cases that may be true, but the reading I've
done this semester shows how Jewish mysticism developed
through history as a way of enabling Jews to persevere in the
face of tremendous economic and political injustice. Today in
the United States, things are different. Jews are a relatively

affluent, well-educated, and well-respected religious minority. But mysticism is flowering now in a way that is still connected to human need. Jews like me are turning to mysticism because mysticism is about finding God in relationships with others, and finding the inspiration to make the world a better place. Rabbi Schneiderman talks a lot about the experience of God celebrated in Jewish mysticism, and shows how this experience can motivate social action and social change.

"He says that experiencing God is experiencing connectedness," Sarah went on, "connectedness to other people and to the vitality of life. This experience is joyful and liberating. And in addition to being something you seek out for personal satisfaction and fulfillment, it can also change your whole attitude toward society and your willingness to contribute to its betterment. The experience of connectedness is a kind of revelation of what human life can be, and stands in clear contrast to the alienation and loneliness that many people feel. It works as a critique of the institutions and social structures that perpetuate alienation and injustice, and as an experiential base for imagining better social alternatives. As Rabbi Schneiderman explains it, the experience of connectedness is a healing event, and it works through individuals and their communities to transform and redeem the world."

Commitment to social justice is one part of Rabbi Schneiderman's teaching that Sarah is already familiar with as a result of her upbringing in a liberal Jewish household. Her parents are deeply concerned with social justice issues — her mother is a social worker who serves on the Mayor's Commission for Better Care for the Elderly and her father is a sociologist who studies the effect of social stereotypes on hiring and wages. Her parents understand their concerns for social justice as expressions of their Jewish identity and they believe that Judaism has been the world's most important source of ideas about social justice. They have often pointed out to Sarah that justice is the underlying ethical standard in many Jewish stories, and that the history of persecution that Jews have suffered has led them to appreciate the need for justice in the world. But they have often described themselves as not being *religious* Jews. They have had little interest in the elaborate ritualism associated with adherence to Jewish law, or in the supernatural aspects of Jewish belief. They rely on human reason, human feeling, and scientific study to determine how they should live their lives. And they are proud of the many contributions to civilization that Jewish thinkers and Jewish activists have made.

Because of her upbringing, Sarah had never given much thought to the mystical aspect of Judaism, or known much about it. But there were a few episodes in her past where she had brushed against this side of Judaism, and her exposure to the Jewish mysticism in college has brought memories of those episodes flooding back. Especially strong is her memory of the day she visited the *rebbe*, or spiritual master, in a community of Jews known as *Hasidim*, or fervent lovers of God. The rebbe was distantly related to her aunt Faye, who was married to her father's brother Jacob. When Sarah was five or six, Aunt Faye and Uncle Jacob prevailed upon Sarah's parents to let her go with them to visit the rebbe. She would never forget walking up the narrow steps into the room where the old man, dressed entirely in black and attended by some of his followers, sat in a chair waiting for them. His forehead and cheeks were very wrinkled and when he looked at Sarah his whole face smiled. His dark eyes shown like magical jewels, and seemed to reveal an inner world of joy and light. As a child, Sarah had wondered if the rebbe was God.

In his talks on Jewish mysticism, Rabbi Schneiderman described the experience of being in the presence of God as such an available thing, if your heart and mind were open, that Sarah now considered her memory of God's presence shining through the eyes of the Hasidic rebbe to be her first mystical experience. She had felt, in that wonderful moment, a strong sense of trust and acceptance and happiness. Her usual shyness and sense of awkwardness had just fallen off like the old winter coat she sometimes dropped on the floor when she came home. She remembered smiling back at the rebbe, and sensing his gladness, and the kindness in the room. She had felt completely at home.

Sarah interprets the mysticism of the Hasidim in terms of emotional fulfillment, interpersonal connectedness, and her own pride in Jewish history. This interpretation is based partly in theorics of psychological development and therapy she has learned from Rabbi Schneiderman and from Michael Lerner's book *Jewish Renewal: A Path to Healing and Transformation*. Lerner holds Ph.D.'s in philosophy and clinical psychology, and is eager to redefine the supernatural and magical events associated with Jewish mysticism as emotionally and intellectually transformative events. While this psychological interpretation makes Jewish mysticism a usable source of inspiration for Jews who feel at home in the mainstream currents of American intellectual life today, and provides a basis for what Lerner calls the "Jewish Renewal Movement," it separates them from today's Hasidim, whose interpretations of the lore of Jewish mysticism are far more literal.

Michael Lerner, Rabbi Schneiderman, and their students differ in a number of important ways from members of Hasidic sects whose black garments and men's long side-braids clearly set them apart from other Americans, and from other Jews. While Rabbi Schneiderman and his students identify with many aspects of mainstream American culture and do not visibly stand out from middle-class Americans who belong to other religious or ethnic groups, they celebrate Hasidim for the delight in God that Hasidim celebrate, for the stories about wonder-working saints and simple people loved by God that characterize Hasidic culture, and for the role that Hasidim have played in carrying Jewish mysticism into the modern age.

Hasidic interest in mystical communion with God revolves around stories about rebbes, or spiritual masters, who exemplify the joyful love of God to which every Hasid aspires. Every Hasid has a rebbe, and every rebbe can trace his own rebbe's lineage of piety, miracles, and mystical enlightenment back to the *Baal Shem Tov*, or Master of the Good Name. Born in Poland around 1700 and orphaned at a young age, the Baal Shem Tov lived in poverty and obscurity until his thirty-sixth year, when he experienced the beauty of God with such intensity that his body was said to have become flooded with light. News of his sanctity spread as he traveled from town to town in central and eastern Europe. Intent on opening a new way to God for poor Jews, he danced and sang about the beauty of God and the gladness of serving God. He was renowned for performing miracles, often healing the sick and rewarding the faithful with unexpected wealth. For example, when he asked one of his penniless listeners for money to buy a drink after the last Sabbath meal, one young man was so eager to please his beloved master that, against all reason, he dug his hand into his pocket hopefully, and pulled out a coin.

In central and eastern Europe during the time of the Baal Shem Tov, Jews were divided from one another by education and wealth. Poor Jews were subject to economic oppressions that made basic survival a challenge, and they suffered the greatest amount of discrimination and persecution from Christians who suspected all Jews of dark crimes and a heinous thirst for blood. Poor Jews were also estranged from Jewish religious life because *rabbis*, or learned teachers of Jewish law, tended to be allied with the Jewish elite, and preoccupied with the interpretation and observance of technical aspects of Jewish law. In this situation of economic desperation, political marginalization, and religious impoverishment, the Baal Shem Tov's message of joy and redemption spread like wildfire. As Elie Wiesel writes about the impact of the Baal Shem Tov in his book *Souls on Fire*, "When he died in 1760, twenty-four years after his revelation, there remained in Central and Eastern Europe not a single Jewish town that was left unaffected. He had been the spark without which thousands of families would have succumbed to gloom and hopelessness—and the spark had fanned itself into a huge flame that tore into the darkness."

In *Night*, an account of his incarceration at Auschwitz during World War II, Wiesel recalls the attempts some prisoners made to find relief from the nightmare existence of the death camps in Hasidic songs. "In the evening, lying on our beds, we would try to sing some of the Hasidic melodies, and Akiba Drumer would break our hearts with his deep, solemn voice." But Wiesel could not accept the explanation that Drumer and other Hasidim offered about why God allowed the Nazis to send the Jews to death camps. "Akiba Drumer said: 'God is testing us. He wants to find out whether we can dominate our base instincts and kill the Satan within us. We have no right to despair. And if he punishes us relentlessly, it's a sign that He loves us all the more.'"

Michael Lerner also argues against this kind of explanation of evil. For a more convincing answer to the question of why God allowed the Nazi persecution of Jews, he looks to an older strain of Jewish mysticism promulgated by the sixteenth-century thinker Isaac Luria. Luria, who was born in Jerusalem, lived in Cairo, and died in Spain, formulated a set of concepts that many Jews since the sixteenth century have invoked as a way of understanding the relationship between the God they loved and the sufferings they endured as Jews. These ideas exerted significant influence on Hasidism, although they were overlooked by the Hasidim whom Elie Wiesel remembered from Auschwitz.

Through the concept of *tzimtzum*, Luria described how God voluntarily withdrew into himself in order to leave space for human beings to develop their humanity. Only by having freedom to err and do wrong, Luria believed, would human beings learn about the nature and importance of goodness. Through a second concept of *shevirat hakelim*, Luria described the "broken vessels" of divine light of God that coincided with Adam's fall into sin. While the presence of God was no longer intact after this breaking, sparks of divine light were scattered everywhere, and this scattering promised redemption, even in the most infernal places, where light had never before reached. Through a third and final concept of *tikkun*, which referred to the in-gathering of the sparks, Luria described the restoration of the wholeness of divine light as a process in which human beings were centrally involved. As the fire inside them spread to others, mystics lit by sparks of divine love were principal agents in the historical and cosmic process of world redemption.

The teachings of Isaac Luria are an important part of the *Kabbalah*, the oral and literary tradition of Jewish mysticism. The most central and well-known literary work in this tradition is the *Sefer HaZohar*, or "Book of Splendor," which was probably written in Spain at the end of the thirteenth century by Rabbi Moses de Leon. As explained in the *Zohar*, the Kabbalah is based on the idea of a secret Torah lying behind the written Torah revered in rabbinic Judaism. The secret Torah is the name of God, which precedes and contains all created existence. (The Baal Shem Tov, or Master of the Good Name, derived his name from his reputation for knowledge of the secret Torah, or name of God.) The secret Torah is also God's *sefiroth*, or creative emanations, which are expressions of God's name. The sefiroth constitute a kind of divine organism comprising all the powers of being in communication with one another. The sefiroth and the thirty-two paths among its parts constitute the *Adam Kadmon*, or Tree of Life. The life of this organism is described in many different ways, often with rich imagery and fanciful allegory. Thus the *Zohar* compares the Torah to "a beautiful and stately maiden, who is secluded in an isolated chamber of a palace, and has a lover of whose existence she alone knows." And the psalmist David of the written Torah stands for the David of the inner Torah or Divine Presence, whose "head is a golden skull embellished with seven gold ornaments," and whose "surpassingly fair eyes ... cause God's heart, so to speak, to be pierced with shafts of celestial affection."

In the religious studies class he teaches at Sarah's college, Rabbi Schneiderman compares the interpretation of Kabbalah in the Jewish Renewal Movement with its interpretations in Hasidism, pointing out that while mysticism had functioned to kindle hope in a persecuted religious minority in eastern and central Europe before the Second World War, it can now function to inspire personal growth and public leadership among members of a religious minority with many opportunities for advancement and success in American culture. Like Michael Lerner, he is particularly interested in the movement of mysticism from the margins to the mainstreams of Jewish culture in the United States, and in the relative ease with which the Jewish Renewal Movement bridges deep historical tensions between mystical Judaism and rabbinic Judaism.

Historically, the Kabbalah has existed in some tension with rabbinic Judaism, which focuses on *halakah*, the tradition of Jewish law written in the Torah and its rabbinic commentaries. While the secret Torah of the Kabbalists was apprehended through intuition, imagination, and faith, the written Torah and its rabbinic commentaries were interpreted by highly educated teachers trained in rational debate and argumentation. Adding to this difference, rabbinic Judaism steered firmly away from images of God and sharply distinguished the inscrutable and transcendent nature of God from that of his creatures. In contrast, the Kabbalah gloried in images of God drawn from the natural world. Until the advent of Hasidism in the eighteenth century, the Kabbalah was largely controlled by rabbinic scholars who made study of Kabbalah a privilege reserved for rabbis steeped in halakah. The Baal Shem Tov and his followers drew the Kabbalah away from rabbinic control. Not that they were disrespectful of halakah, or uncommitted to ritual observances that set them apart as Jews. But with the Hasidim, the Kabbalah became an alternative to rabbinic Judaism—a form of popular religion defined by and for the common people.

Sarah's interest in both studying the Kabbalah and attending rabbinical school reflects the emergence of new interest in the relationship between Jewish mysticism and Jewish law, and the freedom many liberal Jews feel about appropriating selected aspects of Jewish traditions and interpreting these aspects in light of their own needs and concerns. But while liberal Jews justify this sense of freedom by locating it in context of the concern for interpretation that has always been part of Judaism, Orthodox Jews are more concerned with conforming to both the letter and the spirit of the Torah than with reinterpreting it in the light of contemporary concerns. As a woman, Sarah would not even be admitted to an Orthodox seminary for advanced rabbinical study, and her belief that her sex should not disqualify her from studying either halakah or the Kabbalah would be regarded by many Orthodox Jews as an example of the violation of halakah that has become commonplace among nontraditional Jews. While liberal Jews tend to welcome new ways of interpreting and combining old traditions, Orthodox Jews might regard Sarah's understanding of both the Kabbalah and halakah as inauthentic.

The openness to psychological interpretation of mystical experience in Sarah's religion can be compared with David Kim's understanding of Christian grace. As described in the last chapter on Presbyterian experience, David's tendency to think about grace in relational terms closely parallels Sarah's understanding of mystical experience as connectedness. As a conservative Christian who believes in the literal truth of the Bible, David is more concerned than Sarah about the danger of reducing grace to psychological terms, and more invested in retaining a supernatural understanding of both the origin and nature of grace. But his willingness to find grace in an encounter on the street, and his sensitivity to the emotional impact of his words and facial expressions, are similar to Sarah's interpretation of her encounter with the Hasidic rebbe. Both Sarah and David locate their experience of grace in feelings of connectedness with others.

The experiences of God that Sarah celebrates can also be compared to the experiences of spiritual empowerment that Lakota sun dancers seek through ordeals of self-sacrifice. In both cases, individuals link their beliefs in divine reality with experiences that infuse them with inner strength, happiness, and vitality. In addition, these individuals are, in both cases, motivated to use the spiritual power they experience in behalf of others. Thus Sarah associates her experience of grace with the concept of tikkun, or restoration of the cosmic wholeness of divine light, and she understands her experience as part of a historical process of bringing about health and justice in the world. Lakota self-sacrifice also involves a philanthropic impulse of universal reach, with its concern for the well-being of the earth, and for the reestablishment of right relations between humans and other creatures of the earth.

This sense of responsibility for channeling the power derived from religious experience toward others is, in both cases, linked to loyalty to a particular religious community. While Sarah's concept of tikkun definitely has a universalist aspect, it is also rooted in lessons derived from the history of Jewish suffering, and builds on a long-standing Jewish tradition of investment in Jewish community life. Similarly, Lakota sun dancers believe that their religious responsibilities stretch beyond their own community, but the main purpose of Lakota self-sacrifice is to serve the Lakota community. Everyone who attends a sun dance knows that the spiritual power individuals derive through ordeals of self-sacrifice belongs, ultimately, to the community. In both the Jewish Renewal Movement and in the Lakota sun dance, experiences of spiritual empowerment function as means of healing, overcoming suffering, and building community strength.

SUGGESTIONS FOR FURTHER READING

Dan Ben-Amos and Jerome R. Mintz, trans. and eds., *In Praise of the Baal Shem Tov: The Earliest Collection of Legends about the Founder of Hasidism* (Bloomington: Indiana University Press, 1970).

Michael Lerner, *Jewish Renewal: A Path to Healing and Transformation* (New York: G.P. Putnam's Sons, 1994).

Mordechai Rotenberg, *Dialogue with Deviance: The Hasidic Ethic and the Theory of Social Contraction* (Philadelphia: Institute for the Study of Human Issues, 1983).

Gershom G. Scholem, *On the Kabbalah and Its Symbolism*, trans. Ralph Manheim (New York: Schocken Books, 1972; orig. 1965).

Gershom G. Scholem, ed., *Zohar, The Book of Splendor: Basic Readings from the Kabbalah* (New York: Schocken Books, 1972; orig. 1949).

Tikkun Magazine: A Bimonthly Jewish Critique of Politics, Culture, and Society.

Elie Wiesel, *Night*, trans. Stella Rodway (New York: Bantam Books, 1986; orig. 1960).

Elie Wiesel, *Souls on Fire: Portraits and Legends of Hasidic Masters*, trans. Marion Wiesel (New York: Vintage Books, 1973; orig. 1972).

10

Islamic Jihad

Attallah converted to Islam during the last semester of her senior year at a traditionally black college in the southeastern United States. When she informed her parents of her conversion to Islam, they respected her decision, but worried that she was acting impulsively. William and Rebecca Benson had worked hard to give their daughter the education and self-esteem they knew she needed to succeed in the world. They worried that she was going off into a radical religious sect on the margins of American society, and that she would close herself off from the opportunities within mainstream American culture that they had helped create for her.

Of course the Bensons were aware that Islam was a great world religion, second only to Christianity in number of adherents worldwide. And they were aware that, like Christianity, Islam has different branches and draws many different types of people, the vast majority of whom are peace-loving. But like everyone else who followed the news media, they were also aware of the existence of Islamic Fundamentalists in the

Middle East whose militant hatred of western culture was fueled by their belief that God commanded them to undertake holy wars against those they believed to be God's enemies. As African Americans, they were even more aware of the dislike for American culture expressed by Louis Farakhan, the leader of the African-American sect known as the Nation of Islam, and his condemnation of Christianity as a racist religion. The Bensons were certainly sensitive to the racism that still pervaded some corners of American society, and they were aware of the tendency racists had to invoke certain passages in the Christian Bible to justify their bigotry. But they were proud of the progress made during their lifetimes toward fair treatment of blacks in this country, and they believed that Judaeo-Christian concepts of justice and equality before God had contributed to that progress.

The Bensons were Lutherans who considered themselves to be open-minded about religion. They had sent all four of their children to Catholic high school, and had not been at all concerned when their daughter became attracted to the rituals of the Catholic Church, and to the spirituality of several of the religious sisters who taught at the school. But during the last three months, when their daughter talked with them over the phone about her interest in Islam, they had become apprehensive because so much of what they heard about Islam was associated either with Middle Eastern Fundamentalism or with black hostility to whites. So when their daughter announced her conversion to Islam, and changed her name to Attallah, which means "Gift of God" in Arabic, they were very concerned. They canceled their plans for the weekend, and drove to the college for a talk with their daughter.

Attallah met them wearing a long skirt, a big sweater, and a *hajib*, or head scarf covering her hair and neck. She was happy to see them, and gave them both hugs and kisses when they arrived. She looked radiant. She was beautiful, healthy, and happy, and just seeing her made her parents feel relief. They had been afraid that she would look pinched and angry or be spaced out and brainwashed.

Attallah brought her parents into her dorm room, which was decorated more sparsely than it had been the last time they visited. A framed piece of Arabic calligraphy hung over the desk, and a copy of the Qur'an sat on a small table in the east corner of the room.

"That's the direction I face when I pray," said Attallah, when she saw her mother looking at the table. "I face toward Mecca. Most of the time I pray here in my room, although sometimes the Islamic sisters in the dorm pray together in one of the common rooms. On Fridays we all go to the *masjid*, the mosque, or place of prayer, near the Islamic student center, just off campus."

"We drove up this weekend to see you because we're concerned about what's happening with you," said her mother. "We trust you to make good decisions, and we know you've never been the type of person who just does things to go along with the crowd. But we're worried that things are moving too fast, and we don't really know what's going on. Are you rushing into this?"

"I know it must seem rushed to you," acknowledged Attallah. "And strange. But I've been going through a spiritual search for a long time and this year it really intensified. I didn't know what I was going to do with my life. I was struggling with how to think about myself. I felt lost, and without a sense of direction. And I felt there was something missing, a clear spiritual center missing in my life.

"You know, there is a concept in Islam about the importance of *jihad*, which means striving and struggling for God. My conversion is really about my experience of jihad, my effort to persevere toward what is right and good."

"Well, I've certainly read the word 'jihad' in the papers," said Attallah's father. "I thought it had to do with Islamic Fundamentalism and militancy. Doesn't jihad mean going to war in the name of God? And doesn't it mean being so religiously committed to a political cause that violence and terrorism become acceptable?"

"The media has made people frightened of Islam. Yes, there have been terrorists who have called themselves Muslims. But there are also terrorists who call themselves Christians, or Jews, and no one implies that Christianity itself is suspect, or Judaism, just because some fringe group identifies with one of those religions." As his daughter made this point, William Benson nodded, acknowledging the truth of what she was saying.

"To answer your question about the meaning of jihad, Dad, I've learned that there are two main kinds. The second or lesser jihad is striving 'in the path of Allah,' which means furthering the cause of Allah through words and deeds. This can mean telling others about our obligations to Allah, and furthering the spread of Islam. It can also mean standing up against injustice because injustice is not the path of God. Allah commands us to defend ourselves, and to speak and stand up for ourselves and others in the face of evil and unfairness.

"The first and greater jihad is the struggle for God within the self, and that's what I've been experiencing, and what my conversion is about. My first jihad has really been a struggle to find the truth and live by it. It's been a struggle against forgetfulness of Allah, a struggle to stay alert to his existence and greatness. I've been worried and unsure about what path to take as an African American, as a woman, and as an individual. I have been trying to find a clearer sense of myself and where I should be going. Islam is helping me gain this clarity. It helps me remember my dependence on Allah and my obligations to him. Now my struggle to find myself is less confused, less painful, more clearly directed.

"Islam is a way of life. That's what I have learned. The teachings and practices are there to guide you, to bring your whole being into consciousness of God's will in your life. The *Qur'an*, which is Allah's complete and final revelation to humanity, the *Hadith*, which is the life and teachings of the prophet Muhammad, and the Five Pillars, or practices that Allah wants us to follow, all these things help you conform to his will. Not in the sense of making you do what you don't want to do, but in the sense of enabling you to experience the will of Allah in your life and find peace and satisfaction in becoming the person he intends you to be."

"Tell us more, dear, about the struggle within yourself," said Attallah's mother. "We knew you were unsure about what you would do after you graduated. And of course we appreciate that you have always been interested in religion, and that you have always been a very spiritual person. Are these things connected? Is your conversion to Islam helping you deal with your fears about the future?"

"Well, yes, of course. Islam gives me a purpose and direction in life, as well as helping me achieve a more constant awareness of God's power and beauty. Islam helps me get my priorities straight, and helps me deal with the pressures of dating, and with all the sexual demands that get placed on women in this culture. Islam enforces my self-respect, and helps me communicate more clearly to others that I should be treated with respect. I mean, when I started wearing the hajib, the men that I know here on campus began treating me more as an equal. They dealt with me more straightforwardly and more intellectually. No more leering and coming on as if I were available to them, regardless of how I felt. It's much better now. I feel much more comfortable about being a woman, much more settled in myself.

"I should get married soon. That's part of what I mean about getting my priorities straight and getting settled. I mean, I can be a faithful Islamic woman and work outside the home, but I should get married soon and start a family. And if Allah sends me children, then they will be my priority, along with my husband and his happiness."

"What does this mean about grad school in Pittsburgh," asked her mother, "and your plans for a degree in education? You've done so well in your major, and in the other courses you've taken here at college."

"Well, I was hoping I could join a masjid in Pittsburgh, and that the sisters and brothers there would help me find a husband. And if they do help me find a husband, and he's willing, I thought I could continue in my studies until I have children. And when I have children, I'll want to be with them when they're growing up. Any graduate work that I do will help me educate them, and I might also be able to use my education to benefit the Islamic community. In this town, there's an Islamic school, and it is staffed mostly by women who have children in the school."

"Let's go back to what you said about Muslim sisters and brothers helping you find a husband," said her dad. "You mean you won't find a husband on your own, like your mother and I found each other?"

"Well, dating is forbidden in Islam. I mean, there's not supposed to be sexual contact before marriage, and people who accept the ways of American culture pretty much accept sexual contact as part of dating. So arranged marriages are pretty common in Islam. If a woman's family is Islamic, then her parents would arrange her marriage together with the groom's family. But if she's a convert, she'll have to rely on the sisters and brothers in the religious community to find a suitable husband."

"Attallah," said her mother, looking first at her daughter and then at her husband, "we want to be part of your life. Of course we don't want to stand in the way of your having the life, or the religion, you want. But we want to be part of your life because we love you and want the best for you. So, I guess," her mother said, pausing to search for the right words, "it would be a good thing if you could help us become better acquainted with Islam. Could you introduce us to some of the people at the masjid? I'd like to learn more, and I'm sure your father would too, about the teachings and practices."

Attallah's parents and one of her brothers converted to Islam the year after Attallah took *shahadah*, the declaration of faith in Islam that constitutes conversion. The Bensons were first drawn to Islam as a way of maintaining close ties with their daughter. But as their knowledge of Islam developed, they were drawn to its power and beauty.

Attallah and her family are affiliated with the World Community of Islam in the West, an outgrowth of the Nation of Islam.

This group emphasizes the distinctive history of Islam among African Americans, while at the same time working to forge ties between its members and Muslims of other ethnic backgrounds. In its outreach to Muslims from other ethnic groups, the World Community is also working to bring African Americans within the tradition of Sunni Islam. *Sunnis* are followers of the *Sunnah*, or way of life ascribed by traditional literature to the prophet Muhammad, and they comprise approximately 85 percent of the world's Muslims. (Most of the remaining 15 percent of Muslims are *Shi'as*, or partisans of the prophet Muhammad's son, Ali. The main difference between the two groups is that Shi'as invest more authority in *imams*, or religious leaders, whom they believe are divinely inspired and directly descended from the Prophet and Ali, while Sunnis invest all religious authority in the *Qur'an* and Sunnah and do not regard their imams as divinely inspired.)

The leader of the World Community of Islam in the West is Wallace D. Muhammad, the son of Elijah Muhammad, who helped found the Nation of Islam in 1930. The son of sharecroppers and former slaves born in 1879 as Robert Poole, Elijah Muhammad learned about Islam from a silk merchant and religious teacher known as W. D. Farad. After Farad's disappearance, Elijah Muhammad became the leader of a religious organization that supported more than seventy-five temples nationwide, preaching that Islam was a greater religion than Christianity, that whites were "blue-eyed devils," and that blacks were Allah's chosen people. Today the Nation of Islam is closely associated with Louis Farakhan. After Elijah Muhammad's death in 1975, Farakhan rebuilt the organizational structure of the Nation of Islam and took over as chief spokesman for Elijah Muhammad's ideas. At the same time, Wallace Muhammad and his followers moved toward the mainstream of Sunni Islam, and away from the racial separatism that characterized the Nation of Islam.

While Wallace Muhammad traveled extensively in Islamic countries, devoting himself and calling his followers to the study of Sunni Islam, Farakhan's group retained many of the doctrines formulated by Elijah Muhammad. Thus Farakhan's group maintains that Allah appeared in 1930 in the form of Elijah Muhammad's mentor, W. D. Farad, and that Elijah Muhammad was his Prophet. In addition to these unorthodox beliefs, Farakhan's group also denies the resurrection of the dead and the existence of an afterlife, which are important aspects of Sunni doctrine. As an alternative to belief in "physical resurrection," the Nation of Islam advances the concept of "mental resurrection." This concept derives from Elijah Muhammad's teaching that God gave blacks until 1989 to recover from the "mental death" of slavery and racism inflicted on them by whites. Blacks were the first people on earth, Elijah Muhammad believed, landing from outer space sixty-six trillion years ago. The first whites were the product of experiments performed by the black mad scientist Dr. Yakub. The race of white Frankensteins created by Yakub lacked the capacity to submit to God, and imposed a six-thousand-year reign of "tricknology" on blacks. As part of this tricknology, whites urged blacks to accept the idea of an afterlife. This idea was really a hoax to get blacks to accept the postponement of the justice they deserved in this life. While some aspects of this story may have become less important for members of the Nation of Islam than they once were, Farakhan's group still maintains hostility to Christianity, viewing the cross as a symbol of the suffering and death whites expected blacks to accept, and arguing that Christ was a white god who instructed people to suffer in the hope of being rewarded in the hereafter.

As an extension of this highly politicized view of religion, the Nation of Islam is structured, in some respects, like a paramilitary organization. The organization is highly centralized, with expectations for participants clearly spelled out and regularized across local branches. The men affiliated with the Nation wear the equivalent of a uniform — solid-colored suits, white shirts, bow ties, and closely cropped hair. Most men are required to bring into the organization a specified *zakat*, or tithe, from the sale of the newspaper *The Final Call* on street corners and in other public places. A specially selected cohort enter the Nation's militia, called the Fruit of Islam or FOI, and function as a security force protecting the Nation against both external intrusion and internal dissension.

By contrast, local masjids in the World Community of Islam in the West assume responsibility for their own affairs and development, although local imams are often guided by Wallace Muhammad's teachings. Unlike the Nation of Islam, the World Community accepts whites as members of its organization. It also encourages ecumenical cooperation between Christians and Muslims, promoting a Muslim-Christian Dialogue Program as well as other forms of interreligious cooperation. In an effort to combat racism in religion, the World Community's Committee to Remove All Images that Attempt to Portray the Divine argued for the elimination of all pictures of a white Jesus, and sponsored a petition requesting a meeting between Wallace Muhammad and Pope John Paul II to condemn racial concepts of the divine.

While members of the World Community are extremely sensitive to the racism that blacks have had to cope with in American society, and appreciative of Islam's freedom from white control, they are deeply committed to Islam's emphasis on universal brother and sisterhood, and reject the racial separatism that characterizes the Nation of Islam. Thus while members of the World Community are involved in combating racism within American society, and often think of this struggle as a kind of jihad, they reject black nationalism in favor of Islamic internationalism.

The masjid that Attallah began attending as a senior in college was founded and developed by African Americans. But in recent years its members have made strong efforts to reach out to Muslims from other ethnic backgrounds, and especially to new immigrants. This process of interethnic expansion has not been without difficulty, as individuals and families from different cultures have disagreed over several important issues. On one occasion, disagreement arose over whether the masjid should be used for purely social activities, and even dancing. On another occasion, an effort to create a separate room for women to use during the mid-day prayer on Fridays, when the whole congregation gathered, caused anger and hurt feelings among some of the African-American women who had worked hard to build and support the masjid. But while sometimes painful, the effort to work out these differences has been a growth process that participants have ultimately come to view in positive terms, as part of the establishment of the universal sister and brotherhood intended by Allah.

Attallah is enthusiastic about this growth process within the African-American Islamic community. She appreciates the fact that it coincides with her own struggle to define herself as both an African American and a contributor to a world in which people of all ethnic backgrounds are treated equally. She also appreciates the fact that her own jihad as a woman is part of a larger process of an emerging Islamic feminism. This movement invokes the principles of Islam to affirm women's equality, while at the same time calling upon women to define themselves, in some fundamental way, in terms of their womanhood and commitment to family life.

To some western feminists, the very concept of Islamic feminism is dubious because the belief that Islam promotes women's independence, self-respect, and equality seems to be at odds with the deeply ingrained conviction that women should defer to their husbands in all important decisions, including the determination of what constitutes sexual propriety. Islamic feminists often grant men responsibility for making important decisions about women's behavior, and at the same time, they hesitate to challenge cultural traditions that relieve men of certain forms of responsibility for their behavior toward women. Thus many Islamic feminists believe that women are wise to hide the outlines of their bodies from public view because men cannot be expected to restrain themselves from openly expressing their sexual attraction.

This tension between the deep entrenchment of patriarchal authority in Islam and the claim that true Islam promotes women's equality reflects important changes in self-awareness among women in Islamic societies. It also reflects the gains in social and economic status that women are making in many parts of the Islamic world, and the attention that Muslims around the world are paying to women's issues and questions about women's rights. As Mahnaz Afkhami, coauthor of the 1996 *Manual for Women's Human Rights Education in Muslim Societies*, claims, "women are often the center of debate" in Islamic societies today. Although Islamic militancy attracts more attention from the media and is "very sound-bite friendly," according to Afkhami, the most important story in the Islamic world today is increasing concern for women's rights.

New levels of self-awareness among women, and new levels of concern for women's equality, and new forms of debate about women's roles, are evident in many religions today. In the United States, Buddhism is being transformed by practitioners who regard traditional customs of male domination as outmoded, and who interpret Buddhist concepts of mindfulness through the lens of feminist thought. Similarly, many Catholics in the United States are critical of their church's ban on women's ordination, arguing that Christ promoted equality between men and women, and that the ban against women's ordination works against the commitment to social justice that is crucial to Christian life. On the other hand, conservative Catholics affirm the ban on women's ordination, which is based on the idea that priests are representatives of Christ and must have the same sex as he. These Catholics believe that genuine fairness for women is based on respect for their biological difference from men, and for their God-given role in bringing children into the world.

The question of women's ordination also divides Jews. While most Jewish denominations in the United States have ordained women rabbis and revised prayers and practices that imputed greater religious status to men and boys, Orthodox Jews often reject these departures from tradition. Moreover, some Orthodox Jews are critical of what they see as the self-centered individualism of secular feminism and its lack of respect for women's traditional roles. In arguments similar to those of conservative Catholics, these Jews claim that Orthodoxy offers true respect for women and women's roles.

In their efforts to bring together commitment to Islamic values and concerns for women's rights, Islamic feminists are similar to Jewish and Christian feminists, and represent a process of gender reform that has swept through many religious communities in recent years. The effort to connect Islamic tradition with new commitment to women's lives and voices can also be understood as an example of the second kind of jihad, in which Muslims strive to follow the path of Allah in the world. For Islamic feminists like Attallah, this means working to change cultural habits that undermine the equality they believe that women have in the eyes of Allah.

Belief in divine justice, and in the obligation of each individual to contribute to the establishment of justice in the world, is an important point of commonality in Islamic, Jewish, and Christian religious experience. Much as Jewish mysticism enabled Sarah to find a sense of spiritual purpose that combines a joyful love of God with investment in making the world a better place to live, and much as Christian grace enabled David Kim to help others in suffering and need, so Attallah found in Islam a sense of spiritual direction that combines submission to Allah with investment in the struggle for human justice.

The struggle against forgetfulness of Allah, which is a crucial element in the Islamic concept of the first jihad, bears important similarities to the struggle against sin in both Judaism and Christianity. Like other Jews, Sarah focuses on her sins and on her desire for atonement throughout the year, but especially during High Holy Days from Rosh Hashanah to Yom Kippur. And like other Christians, David Kim understands sin as a human tendency to rebel against God and to be enslaved by self-interest. Thus in the sinner's world, the self stands at the center of attention, where God should be, obscuring awareness of God, and limiting the individual's ability to glorify God and live according to his will. Similarly for Attallah, anxiety and confusion about her future obscured her awareness of Allah and drew her away from submission to his will. Only when she became immersed in Islam did she find a way of life that enabled her to focus less on her own uncertainties and more on divine will.

Important similarities also exist between Islamic experiences of jihad and Native American experiences of spiritual growth and commitment to community. Like the ordeals of self-sacrifice in the Lakota sun dance, Attallah's first jihad is a strenuous and highly focused effort to attain spiritual insight and direction. Furthermore, Attallah's second jihad—her struggle "in the path of Allah" to contribute to a just world in which both African Americans and women are treated fairly— is similar to the concern for the well-being of the community so characteristic of sun dance participants. Thus in both Lakota and Islamic experiences, believers strive to establish a contact with the spiritual world that will transform them personally, while at the same time committing themselves to serve and strengthen their communities.

SUGGESTIONS FOR FURTHER READING

Steven Barboza, *American Jihad: Islam after Malcolm X* (New York: Bantam Doubleday Dell Publishing Group, 1993).

Yvonne Y. Haddad, "A Century of Islam in America," *The Muslim World Today*, Occasional Paper No. 4 (Washington, D.C.: Islamic Affairs Programs, The Middle East Institute, 1986).

Yvonne Yazbeck Haddad and Jan Idleman Smith, eds., *Muslim Communities in North America*, (Albany: State University of New York Press, 1994).

Michael A. Koszegi and J. Gordon Melton, eds., *Islam in North America: A Sourcebook* (New York: Garland Publishing, Inc., 1992).

Aminah Beverly McCloud, *African American Islam* (New York: Routledge, 1995).

11

Experiencing God in the Hindu Bhagavadgita

Ramesh Patel has given considerable thought to the images of God portrayed in the *Bhagavadgita*, the Hindu Song of the Lord, often referred to simply as the *Gita*. He is particularly fascinated by the Gita's image of the body of God, as it appears to the Prince Arjuna on a battlefield. When Arjuna's charioteer discloses his identity as Krsna, the incarnation of Visnu, one of the major forms of divine reality in Hindu theology, Arjuna asks him to reveal himself as Supreme Being. When Krsna obliges, Arjuna is astonished by what he sees. "In your body, O Lord, I see all the *devas* (divine beings) and the hosts of beings, *Brahma* (the creator god) seated on the lotus-throne and the *rsis* (wise men) and *nagas* (holy snakes). I behold you, infinite in form on all sides, with numberless arms, bellies, faces and eyes, but I do not see your middle or beginning."

Arjuna is terrified by what he sees is in store for the men going into battle. These warriors "are rushing into your flaming mouths as torrents rushing into the ocean. As moths rush swiftly into a blazing fire to perish there, so do these men rush into your mouths with great speed to their own destruction.

Devouring all the world on every side with your flaming mouths you lick them up. Your fiery rays fill this whole universe and scorch it with their fierce radiance, O Visnu!"

Krsna responds to Arjuna's awestruck words with a further disclosure. "Time am I," says the great ruler of the universe. If Arjuna thinks that he can alter time, and the fate that time has in store for each individual, he is mistaken. The outcome of the battle is already decided, and Arjuna's enemies, who are trying to steal his rightful throne, will perish. Although Arjuna hesitates to fight them because many of them are kinsmen and former friends, his refusal to participate in the battle will do these men no good: "Even without you all the warriors arrayed in the opposing armies shall not live on. Therefore arise and fight and win glory. Conquering your enemies enjoy a prosperous kingdom. They have been slain by me already, you be the instrument alone. Slay Drona, Bhisma, Jayadratha, Karna and the other heroes who are doomed by me. Be not afraid. Fight! You will conquer your enemies in battle!"

When Ramesh hears or recites this passage from the Gita, he is always shaken by the terrible splendor of the truth it reveals. Time waits for no one. Time is the Supreme Being that incorporates each individual life. Breathtaking in scale, this Supreme Being gives birth to all forms of life, and consumes them all. Horrible in its bloodiness and carnage — as full of death and destruction as it is of birth and the flowering of new life — it is also incredibly magnificent — a glorious pageant full of color, story, complexity, and beauty. When this image of the body of God fills his consciousness, Ramesh feels that the Gita has led him into the presence of a sacred reality, and that he is seeing into the awesome truth about life.

Born in the United States as the first son of immigrants from India, Ramesh is a recent graduate of a university in California, where he had been recruited on a tennis scholarship and had maintained a strong grade point average. Currently in training for a series of international tournaments that he hopes will develop his career as a competitive tennis player, he enjoys travel and exposure to life in different regions of the world. At the same time, he identifies strongly with American culture. Convinced that democracy is the best system of government, he is quite critical of the Hindu *caste system*, which still permeates social life in India, despite the democratic constitution of the Indian government.

The caste system divides Hindu society in India into *varnas*, or hereditary classes, each with carefully prescribed rules for work and social interaction. The four principal varnas are described by the *Rgveda*, the earliest Indo-Aryan scripture, as the products of the dismemberment and sacrifice of the primeval Supreme Being. *Brahmins* came from his mouth, *Ksatriyas* from his chest, *Vaisyas* from his belly, and *Sudras* from his feet. According to the lawbook of Manu, written in the early centuries of the common era, the Brahmins are the priests meant to teach and advise others, the Ksatriyas are warriors meant to be kings and administrators, the Vaisyas are meant to be farmers and merchants who generate wealth, and the Sudras are meant to be laborers and servants for the others. Beneath the four varnas are outcastes, viewed as completely unclean, lower than cattle, and unfit for all but the most menial work. The famous reformer Mahatma Gandhi befriended these untouchables, and referred to them as *Harijans*, or God's people. Gandhi's efforts contributed to the abolition of untouchability in the constitution of the Indian Republic, but discrimination against outcastes still exists in India, as does the observance of distinctions among the four varnas and their subdivisions.

Ramesh is critical of the hold that caste still exerts on society in India, and he is not alone among Hindus in his disdain for the concern for purity and fear of defilement that characterizes the religious life of many people in India. Like many educated Hindus, Ramesh considers himself rational and scientific in his approach to many aspects of life. But at the same time, he is deeply attracted to the spiritual outlook of Hindu philosophy. He is especially drawn to the Bhagavadgita because it captures this outlook so eloquently. In the copy of the Gita he learned to recite from as a child, the poem is less than sixty small pages. But it is rich enough to bear continual interpretation and discussion. When he can, Ramesh attends the *Gita Mandal,* or study group, at the India Cultural Center in the city that is his home base. The group meets one evening a week for reading and discussion of particular passages in the Gita, and occasionally hosts visiting *swamis,* or Hindu scholars, who lecture on the Gita in larger gatherings that also serve as fund raisers for the Cultural Center.

At the last meeting of the Gita Mandal Ramesh attended, the group discussed his favorite part of the Gita, the passage in which Krsna reveals himself as Supreme Being. One of the other men in the group, an engineer from Tamil Nadu in the southern part of India, gave his interpretation.

"When I read this passage before coming here tonight," began Mr. Kothari, "I was struck with a whole new meaning. As a new emigrant ten years ago, I have often felt badly about leaving my family in Tamil Nadu, my parents, aunts and uncles, brothers and cousins, nieces and nephews. I have moved far away from them mentally as well as geographically. I am no longer part of their world. There are shrines, temples, holy men, and gods and goddesses everywhere in Tamil Nadu. Home rituals and public processions and festivals are going on all the time. Even though my family was educated and pretty secular in some ways, we still inhabited a world that was saturated by religious images, religious beliefs, and religious practices. When I lived there, I was often impatient with this religious world. I thought it was backward, and I still do. And I still blame it for keeping so many people in poverty. But there's also something underlying all the fear and superstition, something true and profound. And it continues to draw me.

"When I read this passage in the Gita tonight," Mr. Kothari went on, "I felt a little bit like Arjuna, finding his old friends and family in opposing armies on the other side of the field. I left India because I believed I could find a better life in the United States. And I was right. I mean, America's not paradise," Kothari said, and the others nodded and laughed. "But compared to India, this is a land of progress and opportunity. In terms of material comforts at least, life is much better for me and my family than for my brothers and their families still in Tamil Nadu."

"I agree with you," said Dr. Sonja Masand, a psychiatrist born in the city of Calcutta in Bengal in northeastern India, "and I find your reading of this passage quite meaningful. We can love our friends and relatives in India without feeling guilty about leaving them, or doubting that we have the better part in life, at least with regard to material well-being. But while we might be winners in this life, let's not forget the big picture. I mean, we're all consumed eventually. If God is Time, then life leads to death for all of us, whether we enjoy material prosperity in this life or not."

"This passage says a lot to me about my life," offered Ramesh, after a moment of silence in which the group reflected on what Dr. Masand said. "Much of my life takes place on the tennis court, and life on the court is always life with an opponent. I'm always fighting, always struggling to win, and to demolish my opponent. But he can still be a friend or relative, although it's harder to play that way because your feelings for that person can interfere with your game. But they really shouldn't because the game should take your whole attention. You can't play the game well if you don't give yourself completely to it. Some people take the game as a means to something else, and load it down with all their identity and self-esteem problems."

"So tennis is like life," Dr. Masand said. "The more purely and valiantly you play, the better you play."

"And there are rules, which it is important to obey," added Mr. Kothari. "We don't necessarily have to agree with all the superstitious rules that some of the conservative religious people follow in India to acknowledge that there are rules in life. Whatever your position in life, there are certain underlying rules for it. Students must be respectful. Teachers must be patient. Doctors must be compassionate. Basic things like that."

"The concept of detachment is very important," added Dr. Masand. "Detachment from feelings of anger, revenge, fear, and greed help you do your job better. Detachment from sexual feelings is also important. I've certainly learned the importance of detachment as a psychiatrist," she continued. "I wouldn't be able to see my patients' situations clearly if I didn't cultivate detachment. Ramesh needs detachment to play tennis. Otherwise his concentration will be interrupted by thoughts about his relationship with his opponent off the court, or by feelings about himself that are extraneous to the game.

"At the same time that detachment enables us to do our jobs better," Dr. Masand went on, "it also brings us closer to ultimate wisdom. And if I understand Hindu philosophy correctly, this wisdom brings salvation from death and rebirth. In the Gita, Krsna helps Arjuna find this salvation through a combination of action and detachment."

The Bhagavadgita is part of the *Mahabharata,* a long epic narrative commemorating an ancient war that brought India together as one empire. The Mahabharata contains discussions of morality, law, and philosophy, sets down rules for living, and offers guidance to individuals seeking salvation. Although there is some disagreement about both its age and original form, many scholars believe that the epic in its present form dates back to around 400 of the common era, and that earlier versions go back much further.

For more than a millennium, the Bhagavadgita section of the Mahabharata has been one of the most well-respected and universally loved pieces of religious literature in all of India. Today in the United States and in other countries where emigrants from India and their families live, the Gita retains its prominence as the most popular and highly regarded expression of Hindu spirituality. Gita Mandals like the one Ramesh attends are common in the United States.

The Gita continues to exert a powerful hold on people not only because its imagery is stunning and its outlook on life profound, but also because it brings together, in one integrated poetic expression, a variety of different strands of Hindu religious belief and philosophy. Thus the Gita incorporates concepts from the *Vedas,* the most ancient priestly scriptures, along with concepts from *Vedanta,* the systems of religious philosophy that both accompany and supplant Vedic ritualism. In addition, the Gita also incorporates concepts from *bhakti,* the commitment to pious devotion as a sufficient means to salvation that both accompanies and supplants Vedanta. These different strands have often competed and conflicted with one another in Indian history, and scholars representing one or another of them have disagreed about which aspects of the Gita are most authentic. But for Indian immigrants and their families in the United States today, as well as for many of their ancestors in past generations, the conflicts between the various strands are less important than their coexistence and interpenetration. Although the Gita is not without paradox or inconsistency, it represents the plasticity of Hindu belief, and its capacity to accommodate a plurality of beliefs.

The capaciousness of Hindu belief has taken on special importance for many Indian immigrants and their families whose ability to retain a Hindu identity often depends on establishing some common religious ground with other immigrants and their families who come from very different religious backgrounds within the complicated array of sects and schools called Hinduism. In India, religious ideas and customs differ significantly from one region to another, and within any given region numerous sects representing a wide variety of beliefs and practices coexist. But immigrants to the United States move as individuals and in small family groups, not in sectarian or caste groups, nor as villagers sharing a common village deity with other villagers. To maintain a Hindu identity in the United States, individuals and families often turn to the Gita to nurture common expressions of religious experience that transcend regional and sectarian differences. While immigrants and their families find it difficult to maintain religious customs that were rooted in particular regions, sects, and schools, the Gita is a resource out of which they can create new forms of Hinduism outside of India and its religious divisions.

When Ramesh contemplates the imagery and philosophy of the Gita, he feels that he is in touch with something of profound relevance for his own life, and at the same time, that he renews contact with the religious outlook of his ancestors. For his ancestors, who were *Brahmins*, or members of the upper caste in the northern province of Gujarat, religious life centered on ritual practice. Not only were they responsible for performing as priests in religious ceremonies upon which members of other castes depended, but Ramesh's Brahmin ancestors were also concerned with maintaining their own religious purity and avoiding defilement. This was a full-time job, and prevented them from doing much traveling or having much contact with people outside their elite group, who were considered impure.

Commitment to caste purity has never been universal in India, and many reformers critical of caste were born and raised as Brahmins. Beginning in the early-nineteenth century, Christian missionaries from England and America also attacked the caste system. Partly because of its egalitarian aspect, Christianity appealed especially to members of lower caste and outcaste groups, while reformers from upper castes appropriated some of the moral teachings of Christianity as a catalyst for Hindu revitalization. After India won independence from Britain in 1947, the government was organized on secular rather than religious principles, and certain discriminatory practices toward outcastes were prohibited.

While concern about ritual defilement has declined in India among many urban Brahmins active in government and professional life, it has almost disappeared among immigrants from Brahmin families living in the United States, where everyone is impure by orthoprax standards. Some immigrants from Brahmin families may consider themselves to be of superior birth, but they could not maintain caste purity in the United States even if they wanted to, and hence are no longer Brahmins, in the orthoprax definition of the term. It is only at significant points of life transition, such as birth, puberty, marriage, and death, that concern for ritual purity becomes manifest among Hindu immigrants from India and their families. Thus Ramesh's parents would very much like him to marry a woman from another Brahmin family, and have children who will carry on the family's proud lineage.

While Ramesh is even less invested in caste than his parents, he respects his parents' desire to retain their Hindu identity, and appreciates the fact that pride in family lineage is an important aspect of this identity. He also feels the truth of some of the religious concepts underlying caste, even if he objects to the caste system itself. Thus he feels that there is profound truth in the concept of *karma*, which refers to work or action and its implications for rebirth. Karma means that the work or action an individual performs in life has implications for the individual's soul, and determines whether the soul will be reborn as a Brahmin, a Sudra, or outside the human realm altogether. When the body dies, the soul passes on to a new form of existence or incarnation, and that reincarnation is the outward manifestation of the individual's karma, or result of the soul's work, in its previous existence. Thus the soul never dies. The soul is eternal and, ultimately, part of the Supreme Being out of which all life is created.

While Ramesh objects to the way in which these ideas are institutionalized in India through the hereditary class system, he thinks that karma and reincarnation have as much to recommend them as any other spiritual beliefs with which he is familiar. He accepts the principle that our actions bear spiritual fruit, and since many bad deeds seem to go unpunished in this life, he is inclined to think the principle extends beyond a single lifetime. Like members of other religions, Ramesh believes that the soul is immortal, and continues on past the death of the body. If the immortal soul can inhabit one body, there is no reason to believe that, after that body's death, it cannot inhabit another. In fact, what better way is there to explain why some individuals are born disabled, or in desperate situations, if not as the result of a particular fate, born of action in a former life? This view of things does not require a caste system, or any other form of discrimination against people born in difficult circumstances. But it does offer an explanation for why people are born unequally. And also a warning about the consequences of unethical action.

The Hindu concept of karma inspires efforts to strive for a better life by living out one's present existence as best one can, but it also involves an element of *fatalism*, or belief in the inevitable and predetermined course of events. If one's situation in life is the result of karma, it is not accidental or simply a matter of chance. There is a larger process at work, of which one's present existence is simply a part. Thus the concept of karma opens out into an experience of life as an enormous, multifaceted, interconnected event. In this experience, the life process itself is ultimately divine and spiritual in nature. The Gita evokes this experience through its image of the universe as the body of God.

The experience evoked in the Gita differs from Jewish, Christian, and Islamic experiences in its emphasis on humanity's participation in the cyclic life of nature. While Jewish, Christian, and Islamic theologies sharply distinguish human life from nature, the Gita does not. Some schools of Hindu thought stress the duality of *prakrti* (matter) and *prana* (life breath, spirit, or soul), while other schools argue that prakrti is ultimately an illusion or an expression of prana. But there is common agreement among Hindus that all living beings — from insects to human beings, gods, and demons — have the breath of the life soul. While humans and other highly developed beings may escape from the material world and cyclic process of death and rebirth through spiritual discipline and knowledge, the life soul is universal and eternal.

In their emphasis on the presence of a universal soul existing throughout the spectrum of living beings, Hindus are more similar to Native Americans than to Jews, Christians, and Muslims. While Hindus place much greater emphasis on transcending the natural cycles of death and rebirth than Native Americans, they are similar to both the Navajo and the Lakota in their belief that spiritual differences between human beings and other forms of life are matters of degree. In their belief that the natural world is ultimately spiritual in nature, the Lakota and the Navajo are especially similar to Advaita Vedantists, who reject the dualism of prakrti and prana, and see the natural world as the outer manifestation of inner spiritual reality.

While Hindu experience of the presence of divine spirit throughout the natural world distinguishes Hindus from Jews, Christians, and Muslims, there are important similarities in the ways in which these groups experience the qualities of divine reality. For example, a sense of awe before the breathtaking power, magnificence, and beauty of God lies at the center of the experience that the Gita evokes in the members of Ramesh's study group. This Hindu appreciation of the beauty of life is similar to the awareness of God's beauty that characterizes Jewish mysticism. And the element of joy predominant in the experiences of God enjoyed by Hasidic rebbes can be compared to the sensual enjoyment of color, form, and movement that often characterizes Hindu life.

Similarly, the Presbyterian experience of grace involves both a sense of the awesome power of God and a keen awareness of God's beauty. In David Kim's life, the experience of grace involved a breakthrough in a tension-filled encounter with a street gang. The moment of understanding that occurred between David and the young men he encountered was a subtle thing, but no less of a powerful, anchoring force in the lives of these individuals than Ramesh's experience of Visnu. Moreover, both the Presbyterian and Hindu experiences we have discussed have important esthetic dimensions—they are experiences of both the beauty and power of God. Indeed, in both experiences, beauty is a central element of God's power. Both David and Ramesh have experienced moments of feeling almost overwhelmed by the beauty of God.

Experiences of awe before God, and testimonies to the power and beauty of God, are no less important in Islam than in Hinduism, Jewish mysticism, or Presbyterian grace. In Attallah's Islamic experience, awareness of the power and beauty of God has caused her to alter her life dramatically, even to the finer points of removing pictures and posters from her dorm room that might distract her attention from the beauty and power of God, and rearranging the room as a place of worship and contemplation.

Like the experience of God Ramesh finds by reading and reflecting on the Gita, Attallah's sense of the living presence of God involves an element of fatalism — she believes that her destiny has been determined by God, and that her main task in life is to conform to his will. Attallah's experience of jihad might also be compared to Ramesh's experience of the ideal action in tennis that, in his mind, is similar to the valiant fighting on the battlefield that Krsna urges upon Arjuna. Attallah's experience of jihad, especially her experience of the second jihad of striving in the path of God, involves challenging conventional rules of social order that prevent women and blacks from being treated fairly, and in this respect differs from Krsna's recommendation to Arjuna to strive for pure action within socially accepted boundaries of duty. But in both cases, God calls the individual to action, and that action is part of a drama of life, death, and spiritual warfare.

In addition, the Bhagavadgita exemplifies a connection between religious experience and commitment to community life that can be found in all of the religious experiences we have discussed. Ramesh and the other members of his Gita Mandal represent different parts of India and different sects within Hinduism, but they are drawn together into a Hindu religious community by experiences of divine beauty elicited in them through their reading and reflection on the Gita. Experiencing God in the Gita also works to sustain community in India, although there, the image of God's body in the Gita is more closely associated with images of the primeval dismemberment of God in the Rgveda, and with the division of Hindu society into the four varnas, the outcastes, and all their subdivisions. Thus in India, the Gita serves as a basis for Hindu unity while at the same time sanctioning the caste system, which has divided Hindus from one another over the course of many centuries. But of course, caste identification is also a form of religious community that draws individuals into social relationships and contributes to the maintenance of coherent patterns of social interaction, even as it divides one religious group from another.

These dynamics can be compared with the social functions of Lakota self-sacrifice, Presbyterian grace, Jewish mysticism, and Islamic experiences of jihad. Each one of these experiences generates loyalty both to a particular religious community and to a more universal religious identity — thus a Brahmin's experience of God leads to a sense of connection between the particular community of Brahmins he inhabits and other Hindu communities past and present, and Lakota self-sacrifice fosters identification with both a particular community at a particular moment in time and an idealized form of Lakota religion that persists through generations. Similarly, Presbyterians experiencing grace, Jewish mystics, and Muslims striving to obey the will of Allah identify with universal images of their religion as well as with the particular communities with whom they share religious life. At the same time, religious experience in all these traditions can contribute to divisions among groups, even among those who share allegiance to many of the same principles. Thus Presbyterian experiences of grace have contributed to disputes with Catholics, even though Presbyterians and Catholics share many of the same beliefs. Mystical experiences among Hasidim have contributed to tensions between Hasidim and advocates of rabbinic Judaism, and different interpretations of jihad have set militant Muslims apart from members of the World Community of Islam.

While in all these instances religious experience can contribute both to group solidarity and to tension between one religious group and others, more cooperative outcomes are also possible. Thus experiences of grace lead Presbyterians to work more compassionately and effectively with members of other religious groups, Muslims striving along the path of Allah work for social justice in cooperation with other religious groups, and experiencing God in the Gita draws Hindus from many different regions and sects together.

Suggestions for Further Reading

John Y. Fenton, *Transplanting Religious Traditions: Asian Indians in America* (New York: Praeger, 1988).

W. Timothy Gallwey, *The Inner Game of Tennis* (New York: Random House, 1974).

Klaus K. Klostermaier, *A Survey of Hinduism* (Albany: State University of New York Press: 1989).

R. Minor, ed., *Modern Indian Interpreters of the Bhagavadgita* (Albany: State University of New York Press, 1986).

E. J. Sharpe, *The Universal Gita: Western Images of the Bhagavadgita, A Bicentenary Survey* (Lasalle, Ill.: Open Court, 1985).

Raymond Brady Williams, *Religions of Immigrants from India and Pakistan: New Threads in the American Tapestry* (Cambridge: Cambridge University Press, 1988).

R.C. Zaehner, trans., *Bhagavadgita* (Oxford: Oxford University Press, 1969).

12

Meeting a
Tibetan Buddha

Before her encounter with the Dalai Lama several years ago, Marlene had only a vague image of Tibet as a kind of mythic Shangri-la high in the Himalayas, where antique religious rites were practiced in remote monasteries sealed off from the modern world. From her college roommate, who knew more about Tibet than she and took her along to the Dalai Lama's appearance at the university library, Marlene learned that Chinese soldiers had invaded Tibet in 1959 and that the Dalai Lama had escaped in disguise to northern India, where he established a government in exile in Dharmasala. One hundred fifty thousand of his followers also escaped, and now live in India, Nepal, Bhutan, Europe, North America, and Australia. But many thousands died at the hands of the Chinese government. Many others were imprisoned and tortured, and most of the religious centers that once dominated Tibetan cultural life were looted and destroyed.

Although at the time she did not know very much about the Dalai Lama's religious status or teachings, there were two aspects of his visit to the university that made a real impact on

Marlene. First, she was struck by the official welcome extended to the Dalai Lama by chiefs and clan mothers from a nearby Native American community. Like the Dalai Lama, the chiefs and clan mothers had leadership responsibilities that were both religious and political, and they were very conscious of having been displaced from much of their homeland by a hostile government. While the U.S. government treats Native American leaders with much more respect today than the Chinese government treats the Dalai Lama, the history of unjust treatment of Native Americans, and disrespect for their religions, established a kind of analogy between the Dalai Lama and Native American leaders, which the Dalai Lama reinforced in a short speech calling attention to the spiritual traditions of indigenous peoples around the world, and to their importance as resources for the world's future.

Marlene was also struck by a second event that occurred after the speeches were over. She had stayed behind after most of the crowd left, caught between shyness and an unexpected desire to speak to the Dalai Lama personally. He seemed so approachable and friendly, and at the same time so dignified and gracious, that she was drawn to him and wanted to make some closer contact with him. As she stood indecisively near the back of the room, one of her professors entered the room carrying her son, a boy five or six years old. He was really too big to be carried, but his neck, wrists, ankles, and knees bent at odd angles, and it was obvious that he could not walk. As Marlene later learned, the boy had cerebral palsy.

The boy and his mother caught the Dalai Lama's attention as soon as they entered the room. The Dalai Lama moved quickly toward them, and when he reached them, looked at them kindly, and closely. Then he opened his hands evenly around the boy, defining the space around the boy's head and torso. It was over very quickly, but it was an intense, almost magical moment. To Marlene, it seemed that the Dalai Lama had given the mother and child a kind of blessing, and that he had enveloped them in an aura of warmth and light. He seemed moved by compassion toward the boy and his mother, and when his gesture around the boy was finished, he peered inquiringly into the mother's face, as if asking if there were more he could do. She gave a small smile, bowed her head, and stepped back. Her husband stepped out from the back of the room to help with their son. The Dalai Lama nodded and left.

A few years later, after she had finished college and landed a job, Marlene renewed her acquaintance with Tibetan Buddhism through a couple she met on an outing sponsored by the Sierra Club. Like herself, Tom and Anita are outdoor enthusiasts concerned about preserving the environment from toxins and uncontrolled development. They are also students of Tibetan Buddhism with a teacher in California whom they visit two or three times a year for instruction.

When it comes to environmental issues, Tom and Anita take the view that all forms of life have moral and spiritual value, and should be protected. Like other Buddhists and also like Hindus, they believe in the simultaneous existence of many forms of life, including numerous forms of hellish or divine life unseen by most humans. Also like Hindus and other Buddhists, they accept the idea of karma, and believe that each person's situation in life is the result of the work of former lifetimes. This belief in reincarnation provides a religious base for their environmental concerns. Lower organisms deserve protection because some of their number may become, or may once have been, human, and simply because they are alive, and Tom and Anita try to treat all forms of life as sacred.

But unlike Hindus, Tom and Anita do not believe that a soul or permanent self inhabits human beings or other forms of life. From their Buddhist perspective, belief in that kind of personal identity is an illusion that interferes with the individual's ability to see reality as it is. What we think of as the self is really just a collection of various perceptions, memories, and habits, none of which is permanent. The life force, or breath, is not a soul either, and has no more material or spiritual permanence

than the air and the organisms that subsist on air. This acceptance of the thoroughgoing relativity of life sets Buddhism off
from Hinduism, which emphasizes the absolute reality of the
soul and also the laws that differentiate each form of existence.
While the Hindu outlook is more hierarchical and determinis-
tic, Buddhist relativism tends to be more egalitarian, and more
emphatic about human responsibility for protecting and contributing to the advancement of life's evolution.

Intense awareness of the prevalence of suffering, and an
equally intense commitment to the necessity of compassion,
also distinguish Tom and Anita as Buddhists, and contribute
to their environmental activism. They both feel a responsibility to reach out to alleviate animal suffering, and also to support the protection of endangered species and natural
habitats. To these ends, they have volunteered in various ani-
mal-rescue activities, including some involving oil spills and
other environmental disasters, and worked on various fund-
raising activities for the Sierra Club.

While Tom and Anita are extremely dedicated to environmental protection, their commitment to nonviolence distinguishes them from radical environmentalists, like members of
the militant environmental group Earth First!, who have spiked
trees and pursued other dangerous strategies in their efforts to
halt the destruction of various ecosystems. Their commitment
to compassion acts as a check on their anger against individuals
and corporations who contribute to environmental pollution.
From their Buddhist perspective, people involved in such harmful activities are suffering, like most beings, struggling to avoid
suffering and find happiness, and deserving of compassion.

Marlene admires Tom and Anita for their nonviolent principles, their compassion for animals, and their commitment to
the preservation of the natural world. But their investment in
Buddhism did not really command her interest until one fine
autumn morning, when something unusual happened that
led her to think about biological evolution in a new way, and
gave her a glimpse of what Tom and Anita would call a "Buddhaverse." The three of them were out hiking, and when they

stopped to rest on the edge of a woodland pond, a turtle poked his head up out of the water and seemed to look at them. The sun glinted on the turtle's head, and on the ripples the head sent out across the water.

"That turtle reminds me of the passage in *The Treasury of Wish-Fulfilling Gems*," said Tom, referring to part of the *Textbook of Universal Vehicle Precepts* written by the fourteenth-century Tibetan sage Kunkyen Longchen Rabjam. "How does it go? Oh, yes, now I remember.

> If the yoke of an ox were adrift at sea,
> How rare for a sea turtle to poke its head through the hole!
> That is how rare it is to be born human.

While Anita laughed at the appropriateness of this saying as a commentary on the scene before them, Marlene thought about the concept of human birth as a rare event.

"There must be millions of life forms," she thought, "right here in this pond. Amazing that human life actually evolved from muck like this, and that the human capacity for consciousness developed from such primitive forms of life. Even though it took millions of years, it was still an astounding feat."

"Think of all the beings struggling for consciousness," said Anita, whose thoughts apparently had been running along the same lines.

"More likely just struggling to avoid suffering," responded Tom, taking a darker view.

"If every form of life is struggling to avoid suffering, the rate of success is not all that great," Marlene mused. "And even though human beings are supposed to be the lucky ones, happiness is still a pretty rare commodity among us."

"But human beings have the chance to obtain happiness for themselves and others," said Anita. "And realizing this chance," she said softly, "is what Tibetan Buddhism is about."

"Say more," requested Marlene, looking at her friends.

"Realizing Buddhahood and creating Buddhaverses," said Tom. "That's what Tibetan Buddhism is about. Teaching people to become victorious over their own anger, fear, and greed, and over the suffering those attachments bring on, both to themselves and others."

"How is this taught?" asked Marlene. "What is the process? What do you do to make it happen?"

"Well, it's complicated, and obviously it's not easy," answered Anita. "But the main thing is finding a teacher. That's why Tom and I go to Berkeley whenever we can. To work with our teacher. He gives us spiritual instruction in various forms of Tantric meditation."

"What's Tantric meditation?"

"It's a vehicle of enlightenment," answered Tom. "Literally, a *Tantra* is an advanced technique for developing the emotions. The Tantras of Tibetan Buddhism are a vast treasury of *esoteric* (secret) meditation practices that are handed down from teacher to student. These practices require initiation and guidance. They often involve *mantras*, which are special words or sayings, designed to be continually repeated as the focus of meditation. These meditation practices center on the body, or I should say, the body-mind continuum, and are often highly sensual and erotic. Through these practices, environments of perfect happiness and freedom can be created."

"The imagery associated with these perfect environments is fantastic," Anita broke in, "full of diamond bodies and jeweled flowers. The imagery is lush and sumptuous, like the joys flowing from 'streams of nectar when the sun melts down the moon.' It is wonderfully sensual and often sexual, like the divine couple whose union 'melts into red light-rays of supreme bliss.'"

"One of the most common images is the *Vajra*, or double helix," added Tom. "It appears in various ways. It represents the buddhaself's diamond scepter and thunderbolt of compassion. It is also a symbol of the sitting posture that Tantric meditators take. It is a sign of perfection, an image of the body-mind reaching up and breaking into the buddhaverse."

"Wait a minute," said Marlene, "I don't understand how all this connects together. How do lush imagery and erotic meditation practices fit with the ethical virtue of compassion?"

"Well, compassion is the means to detachment from desire, and that's why all the Tibetan sages call it the essence of widom," said Anita. "By enabling you to identify with other people and other living beings, compassion helps get rid of the illusion that you are a separate entity independent of others. Compassion involves exposure to suffering, and readiness to respond to suffering whenever you find it. But it isn't a bitter thing, or something you achieve by denying happiness. It's really an enlargement of your perception of being. And because it's the means to detachment from desire, compassion actually liberates you from suffering, which Buddhists believe is always caused by desire. Being liberated from suffering makes you joyful, and really free to experience the beauty of life.

"Those sensuous Tantric mantras we were talking about," Anita went on, "are really exercises for developing compassionate detachment. If you are guided by detachment as you move through these exercises, then you move through freely, disentangled from all the clinging suffering that is caused by desire."

"This paradox about compassion," said Marlene after a pause, "I mean, this idea that compassion exposes you to a lot of suffering even as it makes you free and happy, this reminds me of seeing the Dalai Lama." Tom and Anita know about Marlene's encounter with His Holiness, and wait with interest to hear what she will say.

"He was so friendly and happy, even though so many of his people had been killed and tortured and much of his homeland destroyed. He was practically jovial. And also very kind and compassionate. I remember how he blessed that boy with cerebral palsy. He seemed to envelop the boy and his mother in a kind of fellow feeling. It was very intense. But gentle, also. It was almost as if he were radiating a kind of golden warmth."

"Well, he is a living Buddha. You saw a living Buddha in action. I mean he doesn't have the ideal physical body of the Buddha, as Shakyamuni did, but buddhahood is there. He manifests a higher realm of consciousness, the perfect consciousness of compassion."

"So it's possible to attain buddhahood in this life?" asked Marlene. "Can anyone attain it? Or is it just people like the Dalai Lama, who are born to it?"

"Well, I guess it's as rare for a human being to attain buddhahood as it is for a sea turtle to poke his head through an ox yoke," responded Tom with a smile.

One of the most distinctive aspects of Tibetan Buddhism is its use of Tantric practices to accelerate the process of spiritual evolution in order to attain perfect compassion in this lifetime. The historical roots of these practices can be traced to two different sources, the indigenous shamanism that dominated Tibetan religious life before the advent of Buddhism and still persists as the *Bon* religion, and the Tantric traditions that developed in India in the context of Hinduism and early Mahayana Buddhism. While the indigenous shamanism of Tibet emphasized magical feats and miraculous healings performed by tribal virtuosos, Indian Tantrism developed as an esoteric tradition of meditation practices involving exercises in both sexual experience and self-control. Tibetan Tantrism is a synthesis of these Indian meditation practices and Tibetan shamanism.

The strong influence of Indian ideas and imagery distinguishes Tibetan Buddhism from other forms of Buddhism. For example, in contrast to Zen Buddhist art, which is naturalistic but formal and often starkly simple, as befitting its transmission through China and centuries of development in Japan, Tibetan Buddhist art is naturalistic but fantastically sensual and ornate, as befitting its more direct ties to India. Tibetan Buddhism also differs from Zen in its attitude toward scripture. While Zen Buddhism is famous for downplaying the importance of scripture in its emphasis on the transmission of enlightenment from teacher to student, Tibetan Buddhism has a long history of reverence for Buddhist texts. Buddhists introduced writing in Tibet beginning in the seventh century of the common era, and much of the early Buddhist activity in

Tibet was devoted to the translation of Indian Mahayana texts. Tibetans played a central role in preserving the classic Indian texts of Mahayana Buddhism when Buddhist libraries and monasteries in India were destroyed by Islamic invaders and rulers between 1000 and 1550 C.E. The study and translation of Mahayana texts continues to be a central concern of Tibetan Buddhists today.

While Tibetan Buddhists clearly identify with the nondualism and universalism of Mahayana Buddhism, they also respect the Theravada Tradition of the Elders, or Individual Vehicle, which is the other main branch of Buddhism. Theravada Buddhists focus on the spiritual attainments of individual monks and nuns, and on the blessings and karmic merit that can accrue to the laypeople who support them. Although they are unlike Theravadins in their acceptance of the principles of nonduality expounded in Mahayana texts, in their concept of the progressive spiritual evolution of the universe, and in their affirmation of the existence of living Buddhas, Tibetan Buddhists are like Theravadins in their stress on the importance of nurturing the attainment of enlightenment through monastic discipline and in their belief that monastics can dispense powerful blessings to laypeople. Before the Chinese invasion of Tibet in 1959, one sixth of the Tibetan population were monastics. The two largest monasteries in the world were in Tibet. These institutions were really monastic cities, each inhabited by approximately 100,000 monks and nuns committed to achieving Buddhahood.

Tibetans view their own Tantric style of Buddhism as the third and culminating vehicle of enlightenment, and believe that it incorporates the basic principles of both the Individual Vehicle of Theravada Buddhism and the Universal Vehicle of Mahayana Buddhism. They believe that Shakyamuni (the founding teacher of Buddhism) taught all three vehicles.

As the American Tibetan monk Robert A. F. Thurman outlines it, the first style of Buddhism (Theravada) dominated Indian history from 500 B.C.E. to 0 C.E. The second style (Mahayana) incorporated the main principles of the first, developed them along universalist lines, and dominated

Indian religious life between 0 C.E. and 500 C.E. Borrowing a term from Judaism and Christianity to highlight its emphasis on providing a path of salvation, Thurman refers to this second style as Messianic Buddhism. The third style incorporates the main principles of the first and second but emphasizes the importance of accelerating evolution to make the universe a buddhaverse here and now. Borrowing another term from Judaism and Christianity to describe its emphasis on the immediate, world-shattering revelation of ultimate truth, Thurman calls the third style Apocalyptic. This style dominated Indian religious life between 500 and 1000 C.E., and was transplanted intact to Tibet, where it survived the destruction of Indian Buddhism by Islamic invaders. Thus Tibetans regard the Apocalyptic Vehicle as the culmination of Indian Buddhist thought, which was preserved in Tibet and further developed by Tibetan masters.

This Apocalyptic Vehicle is characterized by the Tantric practices described above, and by a closely related belief in the existence of living Buddhas. Through the esoteric meditation practices preserved and developed in Tibet, some individuals (Thurman calls them "psychonauts") attain perfect compassion and create environments beneficial for others. The most prominent example of a living Buddha today is the Dalai Lama.

Tibetan Buddhists regard the Dalai Lama as both the rightful hereditary ruler of Tibet, and the incarnation of former Buddhas. Tibetans believe the present Dalai Lama, Tenzin Gyatso, to be the fourteenth incarnation of the first Dalai Lama and Precious Master Jey Tsong Khapa (1357–1419), who is still venerated as a Buddha and believed to have been the incarnation of Manjushri, the god of wisdom. A renowned philosopher, administrator, and statesman, Tsong Khapa enlarged and reorganized the monastic systems of Tibetan Buddhism, and established the Great Miracle Prayer Festival, which drew the people of Tibet together each year as a religious nation.

The present Dalai Lama, Tenzin Gyatso, may be equally revered for his success in carrying the religious tradition of

Tibetan Buddhism to the world, and giving the universalist, messianic, and environmental teachings of Buddhism a new formulation. He is also revered for his determination to restore the Tibetan homeland. In the address he delivered when he received the Nobel Peace Prize in 1989, he announced his plan to make Tibet a world center "for the promotion and development of peace." As he said in that address, "It is my dream that the entire Tibetan plateau should become a free refuge where humanity and nature can live in peace and in harmonious balance. It would be a place where people from all over the world could come to seek the true meaning of peace within themselves, away from the tensions and pressures of much of the rest of the world."

Central to this vision of Tibet is the concept of *ahimsa*, or nonviolence. This concept originated in Jainism, a religion of strict harmlessness established by the sage Mahavira in northern India in the sixth century before the common era. The Dalai Lama's understanding of ahimsa derives from his teacher Mahatma Gandhi, who adopted this Jain concept as a strategy for Hindu resistance against British rule. In the Dalai Lama's vision of the future, Tibet will become a zone of ahimsa, a demilitarized zone that would act as a peaceful buffer between Asia's biggest military powers and as a sanctuary for religious people from all over the world. Known for its spectacular mountains, hidden valleys, and the vivid colors produced by its high altitudes, it would also be a natural park and preserve. As the Dalai Lama noted, "When I visited Costa Rica earlier this year, I saw how a country can develop successfully without an army, to become a stable democracy with a commitment to peace and the protection of the natural environment. This confirmed my belief that my vision of Tibet in the future is a realistic plan, not merely a dream."

The Dalai Lama's Nobel address signaled the emergence of Tibetan Buddhism out of the isolation it enjoyed for centuries into the larger world. While many of the images and ideas associated with Tibetan Buddhism seem to lend themselves easily to global and futuristic interpretation, the leaders of

Tibetan Buddhism have altered their religion by opening it to new populations and new forms of interpretation, and seem to be making a concerted and deliberate effort to cast their religion in terms of contemporary issues and sensibilities. Already, the Dalai Lama's foremost student, Robert Thurman, has created important new translations of Tibetan texts, and made considerable progress in linking Tibetan ideas to problems in western philosophy.

The messianism of Tibetan Buddhism is also acquiring new forms of interpretation in light of the Dalai Lama's efforts to promote world peace, and in light of his vision of Tibet as a center for global spiritual transformation. This messianic impulse is one example of the link between experience and community that has been a focus in this part of the book. Much as the Presbyterian experience of grace involves a missionary impulse for David Kim, much as the experience of Jewish mysticism inspires Sarah with the desire to build a more just society, and much as the experience of jihad leads Attallah to carve out an Islamic path in life that she hopes her friends and family will follow, so the Dalai Lama's experiences as an enlightened psychonaut impel him to expand his Buddhist community as far as possible.

As a result both of the Chinese takeover of Tibet and of recent efforts made by the Dalai Lama and his students to apply the teachings of Tibetan Buddhism to problems around the world today, the relationship between religious experience and Tibetan community life has changed dramatically. Before 1959, the efforts that Tibetan Buddhists made to cultivate Buddhahood and Buddhaverses contributed directly to the structure of Tibetan society and to the maintenance of a national culture. But after 1959, when the religious structure of Tibetan society was dismantled, the social function of Tibetan religious experience changed. Now, the universalism of Tibetan theology has a universal stage, and the apocalyptic commitment to creating Buddhas and Buddhaverses has suddenly acquired a global network of spiritual investors. This international involvement is prompting significant change in the understanding of Tibet itself. It is now, more than ever, a state of mind attainable through religious experience, as well as a geographical locale.

Today, every one of the religions discussed in this book is caught up in changes brought about by new forms of communication and globalization. While their international exposure may not be as recent or as dramatic as that of Tibetan Buddhism, there are few if any religions entirely confined to a particular place. And religions that have long histories of wide geographic exposure — like Christianity and Islam — find communication among constituents to be fuller and often more intense. As a result of these new dynamics, the universal claims of each religion take on new relevance. At the same time, the pluralism of religion is increasingly evident, and even the most devout religious practitioners cannot avoid the neighboring presence of devout practitioners from competing faiths.

The third and final part of the book takes up the question of how religious communities operate in an increasingly global and pluralistic society. The last part of the book will examine the power that religious communities exert on the lives of individuals and on the structure of societies in the world today, and also the constraints that pluralism exerts on this power.

SUGGESTIONS FOR FURTHER READING

Agehananda Bharati, *The Tantric Tradition* (Garden City: Anchor Books, 1970).

John Blofeld, *The Tantric Mysticism of Tibet: A Practical Guide* (New York: Dutton, 1970).

Rick Fields, *How the Swans Came to the Lake: A Narrative History of Buddhism in America*, 3d ed. (Boston: Shambala Publications, 1992).

John Snelling, *The Buddhist Handbook: A Complete Guide to Buddhist Schools, Teaching, Practice, and History* (Rochester, Vt.: Inner Traditions International, 1991).

Robert A. F. Thurman, *The Central Philosophy of Tibet: A Study and Translation of Jey Tsong Khapa's Essence of True Eloquence* (Princeton: Princeton University Press, 1984).

Robert A. F. Thurman, *Essential Tibetan Buddhism* (New York: Harper-Collins Publishers, 1995).

Part III

—ᴍ—

Community

The Power of
Religious Community

—⁂—

Religious communities exert significant power in the larger social world as agents of social order, social change, and social conflict. They exert power in the world partly through group activities that implement social agendas, and partly by shaping the attitudes and behaviors of individual members. As centers for the implementation of group agendas, religious communities work through philanthropy, missionary outreach, political lobbying, or other forms of social action to restore a social order believed to have existed in the past, help create a new order for the future, or contribute to forces supporting social conditions as they exist in the present. As centers for the socialization of individuals, religious communities teach their members to cultivate certain attitudes toward themselves and others, and encourage particular kinds of social behaviors that members bring to their interactions in the larger world. In many cases, individual members of religious communities play constructive roles in the larger society as exemplars of civility and goodwill.

People with ties to religious communities often bring into the larger world an underlying trust in other people that contributes to the very existence of society, as well as to its stability and well-being. In many cases, however, the underlying social trust fostered by members of religious communities may extend only to some groups of people and not to others. Religious communities may encourage their members to distinguish themselves from other people, and to draw lines between themselves and outsiders, who may be treated as strangers, or even enemies. In such cases, members of religious communities contribute to the maintenance of class structures within society, to social tension, and even to conflict.

In our consideration of the power of religious communities, we turn first to discussion of how religious communities work internally, focusing on how they guide and transform the lives of their members. This initial discussion summarizes and elaborates upon themes developed in the first two parts of the book. The latter part of the essay takes up the issue of the power of religious communities in the larger world. That discussion centers on the relationship between religion and society, and on the pressures that religious diversity exerts on that relationship.

Focusing especially on the United States, where religious conflict is relatively low and religious diversity is extremely high, we consider the role that religious communities play in fostering social engagement and trust in a pluralistic society. We also consider the role that strong social and legal traditions of religious freedom have played both in averting religious conflict and nurturing religious diversity. In addition, we examine the increasing independence of religion as a predictor of social status, ethnic background, and geographical location, and the tendencies to individualized spirituality and religious privatism that are closely associated with religious freedom and diversity, but more controversial. As part of this story, we discuss the extraordinary influence that Protestant Christianity has exerted on the formation and development of American society, including its traditions of religious freedom and tendencies to religious diversity and privatism. We also consider Protestant Christianity's loss of control over American society as, at least in part, an expression of its success.

HOW RELIGIOUS COMMUNITIES WORK INTERNALLY

Religion

Religion is the expression of belief about the sacred in practice, experience, and community. Each aspect of religion — sacrality, belief, practice, experience, and community — coexists with the other aspects and is dependent on them. It takes all five elements to make religion, and in most cases, the existence of one implies the existence of all the others. This book focuses on practice, experience, and community because we are primarily interested in the power of religion, and it is through these aspects of religion that belief in the sacred makes a difference in the lives of religious people, and in the larger societies that religious people inhabit.

The Sacred

The sacred is present in all aspects of religion — belief, practice, experience, and community. It is the quality of holiness, divine beauty, or ultimate reality operative in religion, and plays a central role in religious practice, experience, and community. Whether or not the sacred has an independent existence is a question of religious belief and philosophical dispute. The question is a serious and important one, and some religious communities require their members to believe in the independent existence of God, or other forms of the sacred. However, answering the question of whether or not the sacred exists beyond human thought and feeling is not a prerequisite for analyzing how religion works, or for understanding its power. If it were, serious-minded people on both sides of the question would not be able to come together to discuss religion and its powerful impact in the world.

Belief

Religious beliefs are the conceptual component of religion. They are the ideas people have about the meaning of life and what is sacred. Religious beliefs are preserved in various ways. Sometimes they are preserved through formal teachings, like the Four Noble Truths in Buddhism, or in doctrinal creeds, like the Westminster Confession discussed in the chapter on Presbyterian grace. Sometimes they are preserved in stories handed down from one generation to another through memory and oral recitation. Thus Lakota beliefs are embedded in stories about White Buffalo Cow Woman and about the sun dance and other gifts she brought to the Lakota people. Similarly, Navajo beliefs about the Holy People are embedded in stories about the origin and development of the material world, and its expression of the activities of the Holy People. In both cases, these stories are passed down from one generation to another, linking present generations to those in the past, and carrying the beliefs that help define religious identity.

Religious beliefs can be extremely durable. The concept of karma important to both Buddhism and Hinduism has been around at least since the sixth century before the common era. Belief in the establishment of a covenant relationship between God and Abraham, which figures significantly in Judaism, Christianity, and Islam, probably dates back even further. But while many religious beliefs persist for centuries, their meaning and interpretations are always responsive to historical situations. Even when the actual words of religious narratives are preserved unchanged, and written down as sacred texts, or *scriptures*, they are continually interpreted by the members of those communities in the light of real situations. If beliefs are truly meaningful to a community, and not simply ideas preserved in ancient texts and kept on a shelf, then they are dynamic ingredients in the lives of religious individuals and communities, and continually redefined. Like all aspects of religion, beliefs are means of responding to life and negotiating its stresses and changes, and thus are always open to reinterpretation and new meaning.

For example, in recent years, concern for gender equality is reflected in the emphasis Jewish and Christian feminists place on one of two biblical stories about the first creature made in God's image. Viewing the story of Eve being created from Adam's rib as less important, these readers focus on a second story embedded in the book of Genesis about a sexually undifferentiated creature fashioned by God who contains the potential for both male and female and is eventually divided into two equal parts. For Jewish and Christian feminists, this story commands attention because it provides a biblical basis for new social attitudes and programs that foster gender equality.

The Hindu story of the god Rama is another example of how stories can take on new meaning even when the words stay the same. This story goes back at least to the third century before the common era, and coexisted in India with other Hindu stories as well as with Buddhist, Jain, Islamic, and Christian ones. But in the twentieth century, with the emergence of strong concerns for Indian national identity and efforts to define that identity in terms of the Hindu religion, the ancient story of the birth and exploits of Rama has come to epitomize national identity for right-wing Hindus. Fervent loyalty to Rama and new interpretations of his story led to the destruction of a mosque built on a site believed to be the god's birthplace, and to the outbreak of violence between Hindus and Muslims.

Beliefs are ideas that make a difference in people's lives. Recall Attallah's belief that the prophet Muhammad received the Qur'an as a revelation from God. That belief became true for Atallah not as an abstract proposition removed from her life, but as a way of thinking about the Qur'an's growing authority in her life. To take another example, if you have a belief in angels, it will have a real effect on your life. You will see angels, and feel their presence around you. Your belief in angels will lead you to respond to some events with a thrill that comes from awareness of supernatural intervention, or with a special sign of thanks for an angel's contribution to a positive turn of events. On the other hand, if thinking or saying you believe in angels makes no real difference in your life, then for all intents and purposes your belief is meaningless, and functionally nonexistent. Similarly, if you believe in God, but you have not developed it very far through practice, experience, or community, that belief cannot have very much effect on your life.

The *truth* of belief depends, at least in part, on its effects. Belief in the existence of Allah is true at least partly because its effects are clearly evident. The performance of salat and other forms of Islamic practice is evidence of Allah's existence, and of human dependence on him. The beauty and order of Islamic communities, and the integrity of individual Islamic lives, also constitutes evidence for Allah's existence and power. To take a different example, Marlene's experience of the Dalai Lama's blessing a boy with cerebral palsy eventually became evidence for her of the existence of living Buddhas, although at the time she witnessed the blessing, she had not yet thought of the Dalai Lama as a living Buddha or conceptualized his compassion as evidence of his enlightenment.

While individuals may wrestle inwardly with the competing truth claims of different religions, and argue with one another about the relative merits of competing beliefs, people with conflicting beliefs can coexist quite amicably. This is because the consequences of these beliefs are not in conflict. To quote Thomas Jefferson from his *Notes on the State of Virginia,* "it does me no injury for my neighbor to say there are twenty gods, or no God. It neither picks my pocket nor breaks my leg." Religious conflict only breaks out when the consequences of religious belief impinge negatively on others, or when those consequences are perceived to challenge the social order of a community or state. Thus disputes over the truth of the Christian claim that Jesus was the resurrected Messiah arose when the consequences of that belief came into conflict with the social order in ancient Rome. Had belief in Jesus Christ not made them unwilling to perform the customary sacrifices to the Roman gods, and had the Romans not defined allegiance to their authority in terms of the willing performance of these sacrifices, then Christians in second-century Rome would not have been persecuted.

Christians have not always been on the receiving end of discrimination arising from disputes over the consequences of belief. In medieval Europe, Christians persecuted Jews because Jewish belief in the ongoing necessity of living the Torah challenged the conceptual basis of Christian identity, and the theological justification for Christian domination of medieval society. The Jews' very existence seemed to many Christians to be the consequence of the Jews' refusal to acknowledge that Jesus was the Messiah, and that his appearance as the Savior of humankind fulfilled the Torah and canceled any further obligation to observe its many requirements. Offended by the implications of Jewish belief in biblical law, Christians associated Jews with Satan, scapegoated them for numerous misfortunes, and accepted their persecution as a cleansing process. The extermination of six million Jews in Germany and Eastern Europe by the Nazi leader Adolf Hitler and his followers during World War II was the culminating event in the persecution of Jews in European history. Although Hitler was a madman with many unorthodox religious beliefs, his hatred of Jews was rooted in a centuries-old Christian tradition of scapegoating Jews as deniers of Christ, and of resenting Jewish commitment to the ongoing importance of living the Torah.

Serious disputes over the consequences of religious belief exist in the present. In Northern Ireland, religious differences between Protestants and Catholics entail long-standing disputes over land and government. In northern India, Hindu nationalists have challenged the right of Muslims to equal treatment under Indian law. In Israel, the religious belief that some Jews have in Palestine as the land God ordained for them justifies resistance against anyone who threatens Jewish control of that land. One militant extremist who subscribed to this belief assassinated Prime Minister Yitzhak Rabin at a peace rally in November 1995. To the assassin, Yigal Amir, Rabin's willingness to exchange part of the sacred land of Israel for peace seemed to demand retaliation. Amir's beliefs were shaped in response to the memory of the Holocaust, and more directly, in response to threats against Israel made in the 1950s and 1960s by Egyptian President Gamal Abdel Nasser, and more recently by Syrian President Hafez al-Assad, and Palestinian Liberation Organization leader Yasir Arafat. As politicians interested in the development of their own power and that of their constituents, these Arab leaders resisted the political establishment of Israel in 1948 and its strong ties to Britain and the United States. As Muslims who accepted Allah's revelation to the prophet Muhammad, the superiority of Islam as revealed in the Qur'an, and the importance of Jerusalem as a holy city in Islamic tradition, Arab leaders reject the idea that God intended Jews to rule over Palestine and have little patience with Jewish religious claims for Israel.

In the past, Muslim rulers have made provisions for Jewish self-government, and treated Jews living in their midst as believers in the same God, and thus worthy of some respect, although not on a par with those who embraced the Qur'an as God's final revelation. Arab hostility to Jews in the Middle East today is a response to the consequences of Jewish belief in Israel, and the power of that belief to challenge the security of Arab nations.

Practice

Religious beliefs are expressed in practice. In this book, we have defined religious practice to include a wide range of religious activities, from priestly liturgies and official religious ceremonies to meditative disciplines and efforts to inject spiritual meaning in the round of daily life. Religious practices are repeatable activities through which religious beliefs become engaged and effective in people's lives. The types and variants of these activities are innumerable, and range from complicated to simple, pompous to ordinary, public to private, and painful to joyful. Their effects on people are also diverse, but in general, we can say that religious practices are powerful because they bring people into greater apprehension of the meaning and sacrality of their beliefs.

As we saw in each of the six practices discussed in Part I, religious practice nurtures religious experience, and people from a variety of different religious traditions perform rituals and other religious exercises not simply because they feel obligated to, but because these practices enable them to experience what they regard as sacred. Thus sandpainting ceremonies foster awareness of the presence and activities of Navajo spirits. The Roman Catholic Eucharist ushers recipients into the presence of God manifest in the body and blood of Christ. Passover seders draw Jews into greater consciousness of their relationship to God. Salat enables Muslims to be more aware of Allah and their dependence on him. Puja draws Hindus closer to their deities, and to the power of their deities in the world. And zazen enables individuals to experience the flow of consciousness, which Zen Buddhists understand to be ultimate reality. As all these examples demonstrate, religious people value rituals and other forms of religious practice because they lead to engagement with the sacred. Thus religious practice is powerful because it facilitates experience of the beauty and power of the sacred.

As we have also seen, religious practice is connected to community in important ways. Communities sponsor and perform official rituals, teach forms of religious discipline, and encourage various other kinds of religious practice. And religious practices stimulate experiences that draw people into community and nurture community loyalty.

Experience

Religious experiences are the products of religious practice. They are internalizations of religious beliefs, which only become vital when their meaning is apprehended firsthand. Religious experiences can have transformative effects on individual lives, and function as the center of existence for individuals, organizing their thoughts and guiding their behavior. They are events that occur in individual consciousness, and often involve intense states of feeling. But while religious experiences are highly subjective events, and thus, to some degree, unique and inaccessible to others, they have important collective dimensions as well. An event can only be recognized as a religious experience when the individual experiencing it is prepared to recognize it as such. This preparation is the result of exposure to members of a religious community and to the beliefs and rituals they regard as sacred. Even if we could identify a set of psychological or biochemical states common to religious experience (which is doubtful given the range and diversity of religious experience), we would only have evidence of a psychological or biochemical phenomenon and not of a *religious* experience. Even the Buddhist experience of emptiness is transmitted through community!

Religious experiences may be "beyond words" in the sense of eluding an individual's ability to describe or feel mastery over them. But people come to religious experience fully equipped with habits, predispositions, and expectations, and these things are ingredients in the experience itself. Even when an experience surpasses anticipation or shatters preconceptions, expectations shaped by community create the context in which surprise can occur.

Religious experiences can be stimulated by practices undertaken by a group of believers together, and individuals who undergo religious experiences often sense them to be shared events. This sense of participating in a shared religious experience may even lead people to impute their sense of the collective strength of the group to the sacred itself. When a whole congregation of Roman Catholics takes the Holy Eucharist, for example, the intensity of each individual's experience of the presence of God may derive partly from the individual's sense of the collective presence of fellow worshippers. Similarly, during mid-day Friday prayers at a local mosque, the presence of many others engaged in the same religious act may amplify individual experience, and contribute to each believer's sense of the power of Allah.

In Part II, we focused on the impact of religious experience within religious communities, and on the important role that religious experience plays in the impetus for community building. Thus the experience of self-sacrifice in the Lakota Sun Dance fosters identification with the Lakota community, and commitment to its well-being. Experiences of grace draw Presbyterians into church, and renew commitment to church growth. Mystical experiences bring Jews together, enabling them to feel the spread of divine light in their connections with one another. The two jihads of striving against sin within oneself and of striving in the world along the path of Allah contribute to the development of strong Islamic communities. Awareness of the terrible beauty of God revealed in the Bhagavadgita brings together Hindus from many different backgrounds. And recognition of the Buddhahood of Tibetan teachers inspires commitment to the Tibetan homeland, and to the growing community of Tibetan Buddhists in the United States and elsewhere in the world.

Thus religious experiences not only occur in the context of a religious community, and derive from the beliefs and rituals defining that community, they also contribute to the maintenance and evolution of that community. Without fresh supplies of religious experience, religious communities die out or devolve into something else, like a club. As these fresh supplies of religious experience come into a community they bring a vitality that reshapes the community and its traditions. Sometimes the religious experiences that individuals bring back to their communities highlight, refine, or revise certain aspects of community life in subtle ways. Sometimes they lead to a bold redefinition of basic principles. Like religious experiences themselves, religious communities and the traditions they pass on are living entities, not machines or inert containers. They are all unique and changing — always evolving, devolving, or otherwise rearranging themselves. In this respect, thriving religious communities are always being recreated, and each recreation is both a new creation and an homage to the past. The religious experiences that individuals bring into their communities are crucial ingredients in this creative process.

Community

A religious community is an organization of individuals who join together to express and preserve certain religious beliefs, practices, and experiences. A religious community is also an idea in the minds of each of its individual members. As an ideal construct, religious community exists in the minds of individuals who may differ considerably from one another over a variety of religious matters, including their understanding of the defining characteristics of their religious community.

Of course there is a limit to religious difference among community members. Each community will have defining beliefs, rituals, and experiences that individual members are familiar with, and affirm. Each community will also have rules, official or unofficial, that set limits beyond which individuals cannot go and still be members in good standing. For example, one Midwestern Jewish congregation strongly disapproves of an evangelical group called Jews for Jesus, which seeks to convert Jews to Christianity, assuring them that they can retain their identity as Jews within the context of belief in Jesus as the Messiah. While the Jewish congregation is relatively tolerant of members who experiment with Buddhism, and would not censure any one of their members for practicing Buddhist meditation, or necessarily assume that a member was betraying their Jewish identity by affiliating with Buddhist teachers, they feel quite differently when it comes to Jews for Jesus. Clearly, members of this Jewish community have marked out a special boundary between themselves and Jews for Jesus, and anyone trespassing it would be subject to concerted disapproval.

Religious communities have both *historical* and *social* dimensions. As *historical entities*, religious communities have lifetimes that extend through time and across generations. Even new communities draw from the beliefs, rituals, and experiences of past communities, and revere certain individuals who came before them. Many religious communities have substantial histories, and efforts to remember or celebrate events that defined the community in the past may dominate community life. For example, Lakota efforts to overcome their defeat by the U.S. Army at the end of the nineteenth century continue to be celebrated in Lakota stories and rituals, as do efforts to resist being swallowed up by American culture in the twentieth century. Buddhists trace their religious outlook to Shakyamuni twenty-five centuries ago, and follow the subsequent transmission of enlightenment through historical lineages of teachers and disciples. Many Hindus take pride in the numerous volumes of ancient scriptures that are part of Indian religious tradition, and in the privilege of participating in the ongoing life of one of the world's oldest living religions.

Muslims, Christians, and Jews all trace their identity as religious people to Abraham and the covenant he and his people made with God. The ritual calendar at the center of Jewish life involves a series of religious holidays, many of which commemorate historical events understood to be significant for Jewish identity. The religious lives of many Christians focus on the life and death of Christ. And the life and teachings of the prophet Muhammad are of constant concern to pious Muslims.

As *social entities*, religious communities are organizations in which individuals cooperate and work together. Like other organizations, religious communities have procedures for implementing a social order that include means for dividing labor, accumulating and distributing wealth, determining status, and organizing various forms of interpersonal contact and communication. But religious communities differ from other social organizations in the sacred quality of the beliefs, practices, and experiences associated with them. The practices performed by religious communities express beliefs about the sacred that have been preserved over time and have come to be associated with the community's social order. These practices facilitate experiences of the sacred in community members. Through these experiences, individuals come into direct awareness of the sacred things their community believes in, and develop their commitments to community life.

Religious communities socialize individual members, and form them as representatives of the religion. As religious representatives, individual members embody the beliefs, practices, and experiences associated with the internal life of their religious communities, and also translate the implications of these things into everyday attitudes and behaviors. In their exemplification of these moral implications of religious life, individuals contribute to the formation of new community members, and represent the community to outsiders.

WHAT IS DIFFERENT ABOUT RELIGION TODAY?

In many important respects, religion works in much the same way today that we believe it worked in 500 B.C.E. Today as in ancient India, ancient Greece, ancient Israel, and ancient America, religious rituals stimulate experiences of the sacred that nurture religious communities and express their religious beliefs. The rituals that expressed religious belief 2,500 years ago may have been more violent than religious rituals today because people perceived the consequences of religious disobedience to be more catastrophic, and religious authorities may have been less restrained from conducting violent rituals. But the basic process internal to religious life was pretty much the same. People believed in sacred realities, and formed religious communities where they engaged in practices that facilitated experience of those realities.

The most important difference in religion today is not how its internal dimensions work together, but how religion as a whole works with respect to society. Although we can never be completely sure about how religion worked in the past, or how extensively it governed social activity, a lot of evidence exists to indicate that in earlier times, religion and society were more coextensive than they are today. In many earlier societies, religious beliefs, rituals, and experiences worked to maintain order and status throughout society as a whole, and religious life was closely intertwined with government, law, social rank, and most importantly, with the ownership, production, and distribution of economic resources. People believed that religion played an essential role in successful hunting and warfare, the progression of the seasons, the arrival of rain, and the fertility of crops. They believed that favorable conditions in the natural world were contingent on the correct performance of religious rituals, which were contingent in turn on adherence to certain rules of social order. In traditional India, for example, Brahmins believed that their religious sacrifices contributed to the maintenance of cosmic order. These priestly activities required elaborate forms of ritual purification that involved rigid rules of social interaction and order.

Similarly, in traditional Native American communities, religious beliefs and rituals played an essential role in hunting, planting, and warfare. Misfortune in these endeavors might be traced to the incorrect performance of religious ritual, or to failure to observe taboos that preserved a prescribed social order. Taboos against menstruating women touching hunters, warriors, and their weapons were common in many tribes, and these taboos contributed to gender distinctions that were central to social order.

Efforts to identify religion and society have not disappeared in recent times. Both within the United States and abroad, a significant number of people believe that many of today's social problems can be traced to the decline of religious authority over society. But these critics tend to idealize the role of religion in the past, exaggerate its contributions to social welfare and stability, and overlook some of the harmful effects of religious control over society. They also tend to underestimate the power of economic and social trends that work against the imposition of religious control. The sheer volume of economic and social activity that proceeds independently of religious control works against belief that natural catastrophe and social chaos will ensue if religion loses its hold over social and economic activity. And the consequences of belief in a religiously defined social order are debated more openly than ever before. Even in Iran, where strict interpretations of Islamic law govern society, and are strictly enforced by religious and civic officials, widespread interest in more secular and less coercive forms of government undermines public trust, and forces the government to repress religious dissent. Religiously sanctioned forms of oppression are hardly a modern phenomenon — one need only think of slave labor for pyramids in ancient Egypt or Aztec efforts to appease the Sun God by capturing thousands of young men for ritual sacrifice. But widespread familiarity with nonreligious explanations for social and natural order contributes to the difficulty modern regimes have in imposing religious law.

Two other trends work against the identification of religion and society. Religious communities are more geographically dispersed than ever before. And members of different religious communities are sharing the same social spaces to a greater extent than ever before. Neither of these trends is new. Buddhism, Christianity, and Islam have been dispersed across geographic regions for hundreds and hundreds of years. Communities representing different religious traditions have coexisted in the same social spaces for centuries, especially in great urban centers like Rome, Benares, and Samarkand. But while neither of these trends is new, they have accelerated since the beginning of the modern era, and especially after World War II. In the late-twentieth century, religious populations expanded dramatically both in number and mobility, giving many religions greater geographical reach, and pressing increasing numbers of different religious communities into closer proximity with one another.

These trends have affected even small religions that are closely identified with a particular locale. For example, members of Native American religious communities continue to associate religion with their traditional homelands, and with the spirits believed to reside in particular places within their homelands. But as the members of those communities are increasingly dispersed, with many living in urban centers far from ancestral homelands, the religious community no longer encompasses as much of the social lives of its members as it once did. In traditional Navajoland, the link between religion and society was a lot tighter three hundred years ago than it is today. The link has not disappeared — it still exists in some important ways for traditional Navajo living in Navajoland. But as the people who identify with Navajo religious life become increasingly invested in forms of social organization uncontrolled by Navajo religious life, the traditional role of religion as the arbiter of social life has changed. This situation is complicated even further by the growing numbers of people who have never lived in a traditional religious society, but who look for inspiration to the Navajo and incorporate various aspects of Navajo religion into their own religious lives.

One of the consequences of this dispersion of Native American religions is increased investment in Native religious centers by people living outside those centers. To use another example we are already familiar with, the Pine Ridge Indian Reservation is increasingly important as a pilgrimage center for Lakota people living in various cities in the United States and Canada who are interested in renewing ties with the religious tradition of their ancestors. It has also become a pilgrimage center for people raised outside Lakota culture who respect this culture and its people, and wish to cultivate their own spirituality in relationship to it. In some ways, this investment is similar to medieval European support for religious life in Christian monasteries and convents. But in medieval Europe, there were not so many different types of religious centers coexisting and competing within the same society. Moreover, some of the functions of these centers as pilgrimage sites and models of traditional religious life may also be new. The elders directing the sun dance at Pine Ridge are not only renewing the religious strength of Lakota society, as generations of elders have done before. They are also marketing the traditional religion of the community for the benefit of a larger, more complex, more consumer-oriented, and more geographically dispersed society.

Similar phenomena are occurring within other religions. Tibet is a focus of considerable religious hope and concern. While the Chinese government no longer recognizes its existence, and controls that land the once was Tibet, the Dalai Lama promotes the idea of making Tibet a sanctuary for religious seekers worldwide, and a center for the development of world peace. For Tibetans exiled from their homeland, as well as for converts to Tibetan Buddhism and sympathizers, Tibet has become a sacred place. It is the beloved center of a worldwide religious community. The fact that it is unapproachable only amplifies its sacrality.

As we have seen, a significant percentage of American Jews regards the state of Israel as the sacred center of Judaism. Although in earlier decades, Orthodox Jews often resisted any confusion between the religious concept of Israel and the political state created in 1948, many Orthodox Jews now living in Israel invoke biblical history to justify expansion of a Jewish state and Jewish control over Jerusalem. Moreover, many Jews outside of Israel support Orthodox institutions in Israel even though they may not be Orthodox themselves, and would not be treated equally if they lived in Israel, where religious life is controlled by Orthodox Jews. In this situation as in Tibetan Buddhism and in Native American religions today, members of traditional religious communities often function today as icons of religious life for dispersed and heterogenous people who identify themselves to some extent with traditional religion and its proper role as arbiter of social life, but who live in religiously diverse societies and are not themselves religious by traditional standards.

With regard to the question of belief and its expression in practice, experience, and community, we can see that religious traditionalists function as sacred entities for those who support them. In the religious lives of their supporters, traditionalists are objects of religious veneration, and in many cases they figure importantly in the practices, experiences, and communities of their supporters. There are important similarities here to the veneration and support of saints and religious seekers in earlier times and in various parts of the world. The difference is that, today, the competition between models of religious life is more complex, and our ability to pass from one to the other much greater.

A PLURALITY OF UNIVERSAL CLAIMS AND CONSEQUENCES

The new level of access we enjoy to many different religions has interesting implications for the claims to universal meaning that characterize religious belief, and for the perceived consequences of those claims. In its beliefs about the sacred, each religion presents itself as containing the truth about the fundamental nature of reality. Members of religious communities find the truth of these beliefs through their involvement in religious rituals, experiences, and community life. Members of religious communities also experience the truth of their beliefs through their involvement in their community's role in facilitating social order and social change in the larger world. But in societies where different religious communities coexist in increasingly close proximity with one another, awareness of conflicts among the implications and consequences of the different truth claims advanced by these communities may be hard to avoid. This awareness makes it necessary for members of religious communities to adopt strategies for negotiating the conflicting consequences of coexisting claims to religious truth.

In the United States, at least three such strategies exist. First, there is the *neotraditionalist* strategy of devising ways to demonstrate the supremacy of one's religion and to preserve or extend its authority over society. This strategy is a response to competition from other organizations or movements that contend for loyalty. It is also a reaction against obstacles to the religious control over society that members of one's religious tradition once exerted or were believed to have exerted. Second, there is the *modern* strategy of asserting the existence of a higher power common to all religions, while recognizing the enormous diversity of religions acknowledging that power. This strategy is a response to awareness of the relativity and fallibility of one's own perspective on reality. Such awareness can emerge as a response to hostility generated by presuming to speak more universally or as a result of genuine respect for other religions and awareness of the peculiarities and limitations of one's own religion. Third, there is the *postmodern* strategy of accepting a multiplicity of coexisting religious universes, each with its own beliefs, rituals, experiences, and communities. This last strategy is a response to living in a society where there is a high degree of religious diversity, and where human activity is highly compartmentalized. This strategy involves the absence or relinquishment of desire to reduce different conceptions of the sacred to a single common denominator, as well as the absence or relinquishment of desire to impose one's own religion and religious community on the larger society that one inhabits. While modernists subscribe to the liberal assumptions that common and universally valid truths can be found within many different religions, and that these truths can serve as a basis for agreement and concerted action among people of different faiths, postmodernists may work to create pragmatic alliances between people of different faiths but do not expect those alliances to be based in any underlying, universal truths.

The first strategy is exemplified by many Native American groups who seek to preserve their religious identity against the forces of western culture. Some of the spokespersons for these groups argue for the moral superiority of their religions and attract to them people who are disaffected with western culture. The Christian Fundamentalist movement is another example of the neotraditionalist strategy. Christian Fundamentalism is really a controversy, and one of the most serious in American religious history. It emerged in the early twentieth century in reaction against modern relativism and other

obstacles to Protestant domination of the United States, and
had roots in decades of conservative concern about liberal
interpretations of the Bible as a historical and literary document. These liberal interpreters claimed that the Bible was
written by men who were fallible like other men, and "divinely
inspired" only in the sense of being moved by feelings of reverence for God, and able to write beautiful poetry. Some biblical writings were more noble and morally elevated than
others, the liberals maintained, and biblical writers often disagreed with one another, as well as with recent scientific dis-
coveries about geological time and biological evolution, which
liberals were inclined to accept. Fundamentalists argued, with
some reason, that the liberals' view of the Bible as a human
document undermined its authority and status as God's word.

As Fundamentalists clearly saw, liberals were willing to rela-
tivize the truth claims of the Bible. While many liberals maintained that they still believed in the universal truth of
Christianity, that it was the greatest religion of all time, and
that Christ was the one, true Savior of humankind, their view
of the Bible as a human, fallible, and uneven document
undermined the ground upon which Christian claims to universal truth had traditionally been made and carried out. At
the same time, Fundamentalists moved away from tradition in
conceptualizing a conflict between the Bible and scientific
theory. Earlier Protestant evangelicals and conservatives had
gloried in the compatibility between scripture and science.
Thus Fundamentalists were not simply old-time Protestants living in a modern world, but reactionaries who defined and
defended their religious turf in ways it had never been
defined or defended before.

The second strategy for handling conflict between the truth
claims of coexisting religious communities hinges on the distinction between the sacred, understood as the true and universal common point of many religions, and the religions
themselves, which are multitudinous, human, fallible, and
often conflicting in their relationships with one another. This
is the modern, liberal view of religion which emerged in

Europe and in the United States during the nineteenth century. Proponents of this strategy include theologians who urge
religious people not to confuse their religion with God, and to
acknowledge that God is not confined to working within one
particular religion.

We saw a good example of the modernist strategy in the
chapter on jihad in Part II. Attallah believes that Islam is the
best means of living according to the will of Allah, but she also
believes that Allah is everywhere, and that many religions
attest to his presence and power in the world. In addition, she
draws a characteristically modern distinction between divine
revelation and its human interpretations. Thus she readily
admits that some cultures calling themselves Islamic are confusing their own cultural beliefs with Islam as it is set forth in
the Qur'an and the Sunnah. She argues that Islam offers genuine freedom and respect to women, and points out that the
chador, the complete covering of women customary in Iran, is
nowhere prescribed in the Qur'an or Sunnah, nor is the prohibition against women drivers current in Saudi Arabia, nor
the rite of female circumcision practiced in Somalia and several other African countries. In this argument, Islam is the
supreme revelation of Allah intended for all humankind but
often not followed, even by those who claim allegiance to it.

This argument is similar to the distinction between Christ
and culture emphasized by some Christians. In their view,
Christ is the Savior of all humankind who represents perfect
moral virtue, while all forms of human culture are imperfect
and corrupt, including all churches that attempt to define
Christ in their own terms. As is the case for Attallah, proponents of this distinction between Christ and culture view the
revelation at the center of their religion as superior and universally true, while at the same time emphasizing that the cultural containers of this revelation are always relative and
imperfect.

A somewhat different strategy is represented by people who
believe that their religion is true for them and for other members of their religious community, and that it coexists with

many religions that are equally true for others. This point of
view might seem to throw logic to the winds — how can many
different claims to universal truth all be true at once? But it
also reflects the way religion actually works in a world where
numerous religions coexist, and no single religion dominates
society. This perspective is postmodern in the way it relin-
quishes the modern concern for an overarching truth or
underlying ground of religious belief. While the modern concern creates interpreters who approach different religions as
variant ways of expressing commitment to a universal truth or
universal experience of the sacred, the postmodern strategy
accepts the multiplicity of religious truths as reality.

In their attitudes toward religion, many people today
express a blend of postmodernism and modernism. We recognize that there are profound differences in people's gods, and
that any effort to blend them into one would be offensive and
intolerable. But at the same time, we tend to assume that, in
their own ways, other people revere the same ultimate mystery
of life that we do. While only a few of us are thoroughgoing
postmodernists in disavowing any common ground among
religions, fewer still are unreconstructed modernists in believ-
ing that the essential attributes of this ground could be universally agreed upon. Even among Jews, Christians, and Muslims,
whose beliefs about God and sacred scriptures have considerable overlap, sharp disagreement exists on the question of the
relationship between God and Jesus of Nazareth. While Christians understand God in terms of Jesus, Jews and Muslims
strongly resist that conceptualization.

Our postmodern tolerance for religious multiplicity is partly
a result of a mind-set that simply does not expect profound
questions to have single answers. It is also the result of living in a
society where conflict is not usually one of the consequences of
competing forms of religious belief. In this situation, religious
life may be intensely important to individuals, and the effects of
their investment in religion may be significant. But the rituals,
experiences, and community life of religion occur within a relatively private compass. While the effects of religious belief spill

out into the larger society through the lives of religious people, and sometimes through groups of religious people who organize for the purpose of reforming the larger society, the primary effects and interpretations of religious belief occur within individual and community life. In societies not dominated by religion, where the practices, experiences, and community life of religion are not closely identified with either the structure of society or its economic benefits, the consequences of religious belief often do not come into direct conflict with one another.

In the United States this trend toward privatization has developed without any apparent loss of interest in religion. Nowhere is the diversity of religion, and the choices among religions competing for individual and family allegiance, greater. Nowhere is religion more popular, and at the same time less productive of conflict and violence. This phenomenon, the trend toward privatization that explains it, and the postmodern tolerance of multiplicity that affirms it, are the result of a constellation of interesting factors.

NEW RELIGIOUS PLURALISM
IN THE UNITED STATES

The privatization of religion in the United States is at least partly the result of the existence, and increasing pressure, of religious diversity. Religious diversity is hardly a new phenomenon in the United States, but several factors have accelerated its growth since the 1960s. In 1965, President Lyndon Johnson signed into law a new Immigration Act that changed demographic patterns in the United States, and diversified both religious and ethnic life. Between 1917 and 1965, immigration was restricted to national quotas based on the ancestry of the resident population of the United States as defined by the 1890 census. These quotas ensured that 90 percent of all new immigrants entering the United States came from the Christian, and heavily Protestant, countries of northern and western Europe. The Immigration Act of 1965 abolished these national quotas, allowing for a much greater proportion of immigrants from non-Western countries. In addition to facilitating this shift toward the non-Western world, the new Immigration Act no longer categorized immigrant applicants by race or country of origin, and instead established preferences for admission based, in part, on advanced education and professional status.

For much of the twentieth century, Asians had been effectively barred from entry to the United States. But after 1965, they became the largest immigrant group. The population of immigrants from India jumped from almost nothing to almost a million in thirty years' time, and Hindu cultural centers sprung up in many cities where, only recently, religious diversity had meant Protestant, Catholic, and Jew. Theravada Buddhists from Sri Lanka, Burma, Cambodia, Laos, and Thailand established temples and religious centers in the United States, as did Mahayana Buddhists from Korea, Vietnam, Japan, and Tibet. Today, the United States is home to more forms of Buddhism than any other country in the world.

Muslims from Pakistan, Bangladesh, India, Malaysia, Sumatra, and Java have helped make Islam the fastest-growing religion in the United States today. In 1952, there were not more than a few dozen Islamic institutions in the United States. Forty years later, there were more than 2,300. This explosive growth is the result of the immigration of Muslims from Africa and the Middle East as well as from Asia. It is also the result of the conversion to Islam of many established U.S. residents, especially African Americans.

Immigrants from Cuba, Puerto Rico, Mexico, and other North American countries south of the United States have introduced new forms of Catholicism and Protestantism, and diversified even further the already heterogeneous face of Christianity in the United States. Although ethnic and cultural diversity within the Hispanic population is considerable, if they are counted together, Hispanics comprise the fastest-growing ethnic group in the United States. Traditionally, the

Catholic Church has been the religious home of Hispanic peoples, but relatively low numbers of priests and high levels of lay leadership and independence from the church hierarchy in Rome allowed folk traditions to sink deeply into Hispanic Catholicism, and nurtured a range of religious styles and expressions within it. In recent years, many Hispanics have joined Protestant churches, especially evangelical and charismatic ones, and folk traditions persist in these newer forms of Hispanic Christianity as well.

THE DECLINE OF MAINLINE DENOMINATIONS

Along with new patterns of immigration, the decline of mainline Protestant denominations has contributed to increasing religious diversity in the United States in recent decades. The so-called "mainline" denominations include Baptists, Congregationalists (United Church of Christ and Unitarian Universalist), Episcopalians, Lutherans, Methodists, and Presbyterians. Membership and attendance in several of these churches declined sharply in the 1960s and early 1970s, and among those who stayed involved in Christianity, a significant minority moved out of the mainstream. As the sociologist of religion Robert Wuthnow calculates, the ten largest Protestant denominations encompassed only 64 percent of all Protestants in 1985, a drop of 10 percent since 1946. While the number of Baptists, Methodists, and Lutherans remained fairly constant during that forty-year period, other American Protestants spread themselves over a large number of smaller denominations, or moved outside of Protestant Christianity altogether.

The decline in mainstream Protestant denominations involves a decrease in their authority and influence in American culture, as well as a decline in the percentage of the overall population affiliated with them. The decline in both numbers and influence has been especially sharp among Congregationalists, Episcopalians, and Presbyterians, whose churches dominated American religious life in the colonial era and early Republic. Together, these churches defined the East Coast Anglo Protestant establishment in American culture throughout the eighteenth and much of the nineteenth centuries.

The erosion of the authority of these churches as arbiters of American culture was a gradual process, strongly aided by the guarantee of religious freedom and prohibition of religious establishment defined in the First Amendment to the U.S. Constitution. This amendment prohibited the federal government from establishing a national religion that citizens were obliged to support, and stimulated religious pluralism by ensuring freedom of expression to religious minorities. In 1833, when Massachusetts voters repealed a state amendment according special privileges to Congregational churches, religious freedom was guaranteed in all of the states that had been members of the original thirteen colonies. Every new state that joined the Union after 1791 entered with constitutional provisions guaranteeing religious freedom and prohibiting religious establishment. Even the state of Utah, which was founded and is still dominated by members of the Mormon Church, prohibited official ties between church and state from the outset of its admission to statehood in 1896.

The growing popularity of Baptist churches beginning in the eighteenth century, especially in the South, and the explosive growth of Methodist churches in the nineteenth century, especially in the Midwest, eroded the status and authority in American culture that Congregational, Presbyterian, and Episcopal churches had once enjoyed. This erosion continued further as a result of the emergence of new denominations like the Disciples of Christ and the Mormons on the frontiers of American culture, and as a result of the influx of Lutherans from Germany and Scandinavia, and of Roman Catholics, first from Ireland in the early-nineteenth century and later from Italy. Twentieth-century immigrants from Puerto Rico, Cuba, and Mexico have made the Roman Catholic Church the largest single Christian church in the United States. The population of Jews, mostly of German descent, swelled from two or three thousand in 1800 to eight times that number in 1880. By 1917, immigration from eastern Europe brought the Jewish population in the United States to nearly 3.5 million.

At the end of the twentieth century, the three denominations that had dominated American culture at the beginning of the nineteenth century—Congregational, Presbyterian, and Episcopal—had become relatively smaller and less influential groups, with the number of Episcopalians in the United States falling behind the number of Jews, which itself will soon be eclipsed by the number of Muslims. The bigger Protestant groups—Methodists, Baptists, and Lutherans—draw millions of worshippers and exert significant influence both on the lives of individuals and on the larger society. But with the very limited exception of the Mormons, whose religious authority throughout all aspects of society in Utah is extraordinary, no religious group today exerts the kind of command over society that the leading Protestant denominations once did. The increasing diversification of religious affiliation in the United States has contributed to the decline in the social influence of mainstream Protestant denominations, and the decline in their influence has spurred on the process of diversification.

RELIGIOUS SWITCHING AND CROSS-AFFILIATION

The increasing diversification of religion in the United States is related to two other trends as well, switching religious affiliation and combining affiliation to one religious organization with affiliations to one or more others. A 1984 survey showed that 20 percent of the U.S. population switches religious affiliation at least once in a lifetime, and 10 percent switches at least three times. This trend continues to increase. The tendency to join more than one religious group, and to attend more than one type of religious service over a period of time, is also on the rise. Both trends can be partly explained by the rise of religious intermarriage, which has increased over the last several decades as barriers between different religious groups have diminished, and as strict allegiance to any one particular group has declined. These trends are also the result, as intermarriage itself is, of the individualism characteristic of American culture.

This individualism is a long-standing trait of Americans, and both its virtues and harmful effects have often been described. As a nation of immigrants, the United States has been home to millions of people who got up and left their communities of birth and kinship in search of a better life. This get-up-and-go has contributed enormously to the energetic aspects of American culture, although it is important to note that not everyone in the United States identifies with immigrant individualism. Many Africans who came to this country were forcibly removed from their communities of birth, and Native Americans lived on the land for many centuries before the first immigrants from Europe arrived. Both these groups suffered greatly from the arrogant, greedy, and violent aspects of American individualism. But at the same time, they, too, have made significant contributions to the inventiveness, courage, independent spirit, and love of freedom that characterize the American spirit of individualism.

This spirit of individualism has been nurtured by the strong emphasis on the individual's relationship with God central to the forms of American Protestantism that dominated the early history of the American republic. This emphasis influenced the development of other religions in the United States, as well as other aspects of American culture. It is closely tied to the investment in religious freedom that characterizes the American political system, and is still commemorated in the national holiday of Thanksgiving. Thanksgiving celebrates the Pilgrims' commitment to worshiping God as they saw fit, and their willingness to leave hearth and kin, and to endure extraordinary hardship, to enjoy this freedom.

In recent decades, the long-standing cultural commitment to freedom of religious expression has combined with new forms of religious pluralism to create a cultural climate of hospitality to religious experimentation and cross-affiliation. A rich marketplace of religious literature, practice, and community life tempts individuals with a variety of religious symbols and offers a variety of religious paths to follow in search of happiness, enlightenment, or salvation. The diversity of religious products in this marketplace is a result of less restrictive immigration laws established in 1965, the decline in mainstream denominations, the greater availability of information about religions around the world and throughout human history, and the popularity of courses in religious studies.

Upheavals in American culture in the 1960s and 1970s also stimulated the popularity of alternatives to mainstream religions. An upsurge of interest in eastern religions accompanied these upheavals, which included disenchantment with mainstream American culture and hostility to America's role in the war in Vietnam, especially among college students. Students turned to eastern religions in search of alternative religious teachings and experiences. Some of these students participated in the formation of new religious communities, or brought new insights, practices, and experiences into their old religious communities. In many instances these religious seekers have combed the world and its history, feeling free to combine aspects of several different religious traditions, and to create new rituals and communities based on new combinations of eastern, ancient, and Native American ideas. This religious eclecticism and syncretism has become an important part of the religious landscape in the United States. As a product of American individualism, it is a stimulus as well as a manifestation of religious diversity.

GOVERNMENT CONTRIBUTION TO RELIGIOUS DIVERSITY

A less obvious, but no less important stimulus to religious diversity in the United States has been the government's stance of neutrality toward religion. This stance is grounded in the First Amendment's prohibition against government sponsorship of any religion, which accompanies the amendment's guarantee of religious freedom. The implications of government neutrality for the larger society have evolved over time. Throughout the nineteenth century, minority religions enjoyed a certain degree of legal protection and many flourished, but this growth took place in the context of a culture dominated by Protestant Christianity. Belief in the supremacy of Protestant Christianity, and in America's role in its worldwide triumph, was often expressed by public leaders. Thus in 1892, during the presidency of Benjamin Harrison, a Supreme Court justice declared America "a Christian nation." In the early years of the twentieth century, President Woodrow Wilson broadened U.S. diplomacy beyond Europe with the intent of spreading Protestant idealism throughout the world. At the same time, American Protestant hopes for converting every nation, and eradicating all other religions, reached their peak.

With the decline of this Protestant triumphalism in the 1930s, and with the increased diversification of religion after 1965, the implications of religious freedom and government neutrality toward religion changed dramatically. Many of the Protestant churches that battled to save the souls of heathens and Catholics in the nineteenth and early-twentieth centuries backed off from this confrontational approach and focused their missionary work on improving health and social welfare around the world. With regard to expressions of Christian dominance by public leaders, no high-placed government official would ever declare the United States to be a Christian nation. Conservative Christians would surely question the judgment of anyone who thought it was a Christian nation, even if they believed it should be. And many Americans with ties to religions other than Christianity would surely rise up in protest at the discrimination against them, and the ominous implications for their religious freedom, conveyed by such a declaration.

At the same time, Americans expect their representatives in government to have *some* religion, and would probably be suspicious of a presidential candidate who was neutral, as an individual, to religion. That kind of personal indifference might not square with the concern for personal character that Americans are much preoccupied with. This widespread concern for character derives from a cultural investment in individualism, and perhaps also from an underlying conviction that the highest and best forms of individualism involve religious life.

But many religious conservatives object to what they view as the absence of religious values in the United States government and the blatant disrespect for religious values in the larger society. As a result of this concern, many religious conservatives define themselves and their religion in opposition to the larger culture. They constitute a new counterculture, resisting what they perceive as the dominant culture in America as strongly as peaceniks and hippies resisted what they perceived as the dominant culture in the 1970s. But while the peacenik counterculture of the 1970s was arrayed against what it saw as a monolithic military-industrial white-Protestant establishment, the counterculture of religious conservatism today opposes what it sees as the decadence and permissiveness of American society, and the absence of a strong moral center.

THE SOCIAL IMPACT OF RELIGIOUS COMMUNITIES

The beliefs of countercultural religious conservatives differ from the beliefs of other religious groups in the United States today. But in many aspects of their lives as religious people, they are similar to members of other religious groups, including those who feel more at home with both the secularity and the religious diversity of American culture. Like other religious people in the United States today, countercultural religious conservatives belong to religious communities whose impact on the larger culture is indirect. Their direct control over the larger society is blocked by the prohibition against government establishment of religion, which frees government, law, public education, and many forms of public service from religious control. Many sectors of the economy also operate independently of religious control, as do many forms of information and entertainment. The *secular*, or mundane and nonsacred, aspects of the larger society are by no means sealed off from religious influence, as various forms of religious media and religious involvement in politics make clear. But the influence of religion in American society is more indirect than in societies where religious establishment is imposed and religious diversity denied or only tolerated.

In contrast to religious communities in the premodern world, religious communities in the United States today exert little direct control over the ownership, production, and exchange of economic goods, the definition and enforcement of law, or the creation and dissemination of information. But even though their impact is often indirect and subtle, religious communities remain essential to the vitality and well-being of society in the United States today. Among their most important functions, religious communities often play definitive roles in the development of individual life. Individuals who participate in a sandpainting ceremony, a Catholic Eucharist, a Passover seder, or in salat, puja, or zazen often find that these rituals have transformative effects on their lives, shaping their outlooks on the world, and enhancing their relationships with other people, their senses of direction and purpose, their behavior in all aspects of life, and their contributions to the larger society.

Religious communities also play important roles in the construction of family life and family-like relationships, fostering loyalty, shared experience, common commitment, and bonds of mutual dependence among people who would otherwise be more alone, alienated, and directionless. As we have seen, the most intensely personal aspects of religion are neither isolating nor merely subjective, but draw individuals together, forging or strengthening identification with one another. Thus Lakota self-sacrifice, Presbyterian grace, and Jewish mysticism strengthen interpersonal ties, as do experiences of jihad, Brahma, and Tibetan Buddhas. As developers of these ties, religious communities play a key role in the creation and maintenance of those networks of interpersonal trust and cooperation that constitute a smooth-functioning and stable society. They also function as centers of social service and social outreach, and in so doing, generate social trust and cooperation throughout the larger society. In our world of religious diversity, religion no longer dominates society. But without its contributions to the infrastructures of society, through the lives of individuals and groups who inhabit and define these infrastructures, society as we know it would not exist.

SUGGESTIONS FOR FURTHER READING

Karen Armstrong, *Jerusalem: One City, Three Faiths* (New York: Alfred A. Knopf, 1996).

Pastora San Juan Cafferty and William C. McCready, eds., *Hispanics in the United States: A New Social Agenda* (New Brunswick: Transaction Publishers, 1994; orig. 1985).

Harvey Cox, *Fire from Heaven* (Reading, MA: Addison-Wesley, 1995).

Emile Durkheim, *The Elementary Forms of Religious Life*, trans. Joseph Ward Swain (New York: Macmillan, 1965; orig. 1915).

Peter L. Halvorson and William M. Newman, *Atlas of Religious Change in America, 1952-1990* (Atlanta: Glenmary Research Center, 1994).

William R. Hutchison, ed., *Between the Times: The Travail of the Protestant Establishment in America, 1900-1960* (New York: Cambridge University Press, 1989).

Robert J. Lifton, *The Protean Self* (New York: Basic Books, 1993).

Bronislaw Malinowski, *Magic, Science and Religion and Other Essays*, introd. Robert Redfield (New York: Doubleday Anchor Books, 1954; orig. 1948).

George M. Marsden, *Fundamentalism in American Culture: The Shaping of Twentieth-Century Evangelicalism, 1870–1925* (New York: Oxford University Press, 1980).

Rudolph Otto, *The Idea of the Holy : An Inquiry into the non-rational factor in the idea of the divine and its relation to the rational*, trans. John W. Harvey (London: Oxford University Press, 1950).

Wade Clark Roof, *A Generation of Seekers: The Spiritual Journeys of the Baby Boom Generation* (San Francisco: HarperSanFrancisco, 1993).

Robert Wuthnow, *The Restructuring of American Religion: Society and Faith since World War II* (Princeton: Princeton University Press, 1988).

Index